The Game of Life

Also in the
"Basic Manuals for Life" (BMFL) Collection
by Barbara Chang

BM
FL

**Riding Quantum Waves: A 7-Step Plan
for Manifesting Desires in the Information Age**

The Game of Life

An Introductory Exploration
into the Mysteries of Spirit

Volume I :
An Intimate Contact with Humanity
Series

Barbara Chang

BM
F L

DESTINY TECHNOLOGIES PRESS
Big Bear, California

DESTINY TECHNOLOGIES PRESS, 2008
A publishing division of Destiny Technologies®

The Game of Life, An Introductory Exploration into the Mysteries of Spirit. Copyright © 2008 by Barbara S. P. Chang. All rights reserved under International and Pan-American Copyright Conventions. No part of this book may be reproduced by any manner whatsoever without written permission, except in the case of brief quotations embodied in critical articles and reviews. For information, address Destiny Technologies Press. All rights, including the rights of translation into foreign languages, are strictly reserved.

ISBN-10: 0-9792753-1-8
ISBN-13: 978-0-9792753-1-9
Library of Congress Control Number: 2008903243

Volume I of "An Intimate Contact with Humanity" Series

A "Basic Manuals for Life" (BMFL) Collection Book

Published by:
Destiny Technologies Press
P.O. Box 1707, Big Bear City, CA 92314-1707
www.destinytechnologies.org
info@destinytechnologies.com

Printed in the United States of America
by Lightning Source Inc., La Vergne, TN

*In memory of all human beings
who died on September 11, 2001,
regardless of nationality and faith.*

Contents

Stage 1. Introduction

Act 1. Eternal Quest
1.	Older than Time,	1
2.	Spirituality,	2
3.	Socratic Engagement,	3
4.	Who Cares,	5
5.	Word Origin,	7
6.	Multiple Angles,	11
7.	Literal Data / Mythic Metaphors,	14

Stage 2. Common Denominators

Act 2. Guardians of Harmony
8.	Substantive, Not Decorative,	21
9.	Spirit "Lifeline",	24
10.	Soul "Source",	27
11.	Self "Whole",	31
12.	Connection,	33

Act 3. All in the Family
13.	Ego "Avenger",	37
14.	Superego "Conformist",	40
15.	Personality "Traits",	43

| *16.* | Observer "Witness", | 47 |

Act 4 . Energy Pathways
17.	An Elaborate Interweaving,	53
18.	Mental,	54
19.	Psychic,	57
20.	Emotional,	59
21.	Physical,	62
22.	Spiritual,	66
23.	Existential,	69

Act 5 . Natural Order
24.	Growth,	73
25.	Age,	75
26.	Development,	78
27.	Maturity,	80

Act 6 . Nature's Inheritance
28.	Instincts	85
29.	Common Sense,	88
30.	Intelligence,	91
31.	Joyful Play,	93

Stage 3. Our Blurred Dialogues

Act 7 . Stay Tuned
32.	Drowning in a Flood of Words,	99
33.	Cheating Life,	101
34.	Running Life,	105
35.	Resisting Resistance,	108
36.	Avoiding Avoidance,	110
37.	Oblivious Oblivion,	114
38.	Ignoring Ignorance,	117

Act 8 . News Flash
- *39.*   Automating Life,   123
- *40.*   Culture and Being,   125
- *41.*   A Culture of Personalities, 127
- *42.*   Designer Life Styles,   131

Stage 4. Life 101

Act 9 . Back to Basics
- *43.*   Enigma,   139
- *44.*   Spiritual Diversity,   140
- *45.*   Words or Deeds,   142
- *46.*   Game Theories,   144
- *47.*   Factions,   146
- *48.*   A United Human Race, 148
- *49.*   Game Master,   150
- *50.*   Instruction Manual,   154
- *51.*   Traditions,   158

Act 10 . In Truth
- *52.*   No Directions,   165
- *53.*   No Guarantees,   167
- *54.*   Biographical History,   169
- *55.*   Complexities,   172
- *56.*   Fact: Gather / Truth: Surrender, 174
- *57.*   Minutiae,   177
- *58.*   The Contract,   181

Act 11 . Universal Playing Field
- *59.*   Equal Opportunity,   185
- *60.*   Taking Form,   187
- *61.*   Body, Mind, Heart, Spirit, 190

62.	Inviolable Union,	192
63.	Another World,	194
64.	Laws,	197

Stage 5. Our Modern Dilemmas

Act 12. Entertaining Twists
65.	Psycho Emotional, Not Spiritual,	203
66.	Spin Masters, Ad Gurus, Business as Usual,	205
67.	Compelling Stories,	209
68.	Headlines and Snapshots,	211
69.	Hearsay,	215

Act 13. The Games Most Commonly Played
70.	Magic,	223
71.	Perfection,	225
72.	Idealism,	227
73.	Certainty,	230
74.	Boredom,	233
75.	Indulgence,	235
76.	Competition,	237
77.	Challenge,	240

Act 14. Rise Above the Crowd
78.	Care in Living,	245
79.	Mindful Living,	248
80.	Responsible Living,	250
81.	Courageous Living,	252
82.	Existential Values,	254
83.	In the End,	256
84.	Decision,	258

Act 15 . Full Circle 261

Acknowledgement 267

Stage 1.

Introduction

Act 1.

Eternal Quest

*I am writing about revolutions
in the mystical tradition.*

Chapter 1.

Older than Time

Every human being is endowed with Spirit.

Our quest to identify, know and realize our spiritual nature is as ancient as our earliest presence on this planet.

As our prehistoric hairy relatives gazed up at the starry skies with mystical wonder, so began our spiritual quest.

Humanity cannot fulfill its full potential without an intimate contact with Spirit. Without its intimate contact with humanity, Spirit would feel a loss.

For some of us, religion offers some of the answers. Yet, to be spiritually inspired does not require a person to be religious, devout, faithful or pledge allegiance to one Supreme Being.

What are your personal rituals?

How did you acquire them?

Are you satisfied with them?

Have you begun your personal quest?

Chapter 2 .

Spirituality

The premise is simple:
Spirit intimately makes contact with us or else we would not be alive.

We must therefore make an intimate contact with Spirit or else we cannot and will not live life to the fullest.

Life is synonymous with Spirit

Spirit is synonymous with life.

None of us would be alive without Spirit.

Chapter 3 .

Socratic Engagement

What is spirit?
What is soul?

These two words are spoken often enough in our everyday speech.

What is it exactly that we mean by them?

Are they synonymous?

What is the subtle distinction?

Why is "soulity" not a discipline but spirituality is?

How is it that we have a name for the Holy Spirit but not Holy Soul?

Why is there depth to the soul but we do not customarily say the same about spirit?

Why is soul searching acceptable but "spirit searching" might land someone a prolonged residence in the psychiatric ward?

Why would spirit soar, while soul soaring sounds strange?

Why is it that we say spiritual crisis and not soulful crisis?

Given that the two nouns approximate their meanings and "spiritual" is derived from "spirit" and "soulful" from "soul", how is it that a spiritual journey implies personal growth?

A soulful one suggests that someone is full of intense emotions?

And, why is it that their adjective forms are not exactly interchangeable?

So what?

The Game of Life

What is the big deal anyway?
Who cares?

Chapter 4 .

Who Cares

Many of us take life for granted.
We witness countless examples on our nightly newscasts:

Our young people shoot toxic narcotics into their bodies.

On a drug-induced high, they gun each other down.

They indulge themselves in five minutes of street racing, rather than hold life sacred.

In some of our cities, the high school dropout rate is over 50%.

Tens of thousands of girls under the age of 14 are reported pregnant.

Our adults are not doing much better. They say, the apple does not fall far from the tree.

The New York Times purportedly writes at a fifth-grade reading level, to accommodate to a median literacy level of a majority of its readership. No wonder "Are You Smarter Than a Fifth-Grader?" has become a hit TV game show. Might its producers receive an Emmy, for satiric parody?

We have an epidemic of adults who are in debt, unable to manage money and face foreclosures on their homes.

These days we seem to hear plenty of people bemoaning "spiritual this" and "soul that", particularly in certain high-fashion circles.

I, for one, am not sure what they are referring to.

Individually, are we each talking about the same "things"?

These sorts of questions have plagued my conscience for many years.

What bothers me is a lack of exploration—or for that matter, curiosity—by those in the inner circles of spiritual inquest.

If, in our language, an apple were interchangeable with an orange would we not end up with a very mixed-up fruit salad—or at the very least, a big huge mess.

In the case where spirit and soul are not clearly distinguished, existential confusion will inevitably reign in the psyche of popular culture.

The impending crisis is that our complacent attitudes may unwittingly prevent us from intimately contacting our own humanity.

Who am I? "Nobody in particular."

How do I qualify as an expert and what gives me the authority on this subject? "My Spirit."

Read on and you will see for yourself.

Chapter 5.

Word Origin

Although spirit and soul belong to the category of "things" that are incorporeal, we must nevertheless use language to separately name them.

Etymology is the study of word origins.

Spirit (circa 1250), meaning "animating or vital principle in man and animals", comes from Old French *espirit* which comes from Latin *spiritus* meaning "soul, courage, vigor, breath".

Soul (circa not listed) comes from Old English *sawol* meaning "spiritual and emotional part of a person, animate existence" which comes from Proto-Germanic *saiwalo*, of an uncertain origin.

Psyche (circa 1647 A.D.), meaning "animating spirit", comes from Latin *psyche* and Greek *psykhe* meaning "the soul, mind, spirit, breath, life, the invisible animating principle or entity which occupies and directs the physical body." Its psychological applications began around 1910.

Mind (circa not listed) comes from Old English *gemund* meaning "memory, thinking, intention"; Greek *memona* meaning "I yearn"; *mania* meaning "madness"; *mantis* meaning "one who divines, prophet, seer"; and Latin *mens* meaning "mind, understanding, reason".

In summary, an etymology for spirit includes soul; soul is defined by the spiritual part of a person; and psyche stands for soul, mind, breath and life.

Not only does each definition not distinctively define the term that bears its name. The definitions are so convoluted and solipsistic, where a supposedly distinct meaning is nestled within the definition of another similar word. Such ambiguity creates a circuitous reference which introduces vague values instead of clearly defining—which is an imperative of word definitions.

Rather than coalescing into distinctly unique and universally accepted common usages, over time, it would appear that their meanings have become even more blurred. Because, their modern uses have not altered much. The dictionary's definitions for spirit, soul, psyche and mind seem to be nearly interchangeable.

In modern usage, could it be that when we say soul, spirit and mind, we really mean psyche?

A quick glance at the above short list would seem to indicate that "psyche" is the most mixed up word of the bunch—not just as a word but because of its widespread dysfunctional element in human nature. For it to stand for soul, mind, breath and life is, in essence, for it to stand for everything but the kitchen sink.

We know that Sigmund Freud formulated our modern views on the psyche, from which psychology and psychiatry derive. By its etymological derivation, psychology is the study of the human psyche. Therefore, we can concur that psychology does not study the soul or mind.

To mix up an intimate contact of the spirit, soul, psyche and mind of humanity is to perpetuate a mystery which presumes that we may not be genuinely interested in finding solutions or resolutions.

What other groups of analogous words exhibit as much ambiguity, unclarity and obscurity? It is not as though we are splitting hair over a distinction between "dog and canine", "cow and bovine", "earthly and terrestrial" or "cosmic and celestial", for example.

We are, in essence, referring to the most personal and sanctified aspects of our human nature.

If only it were that easy to sort through the tangled mess by tracing the origin of words.

Sometimes the dictionary leads me on a paper chase. In this case, however, the hunt for the Holy Grail is elusive to the extreme.

The confusion is so blatantly obvious. It blares at me so loudly. Sometimes I feel the need to shout at the tops of my lungs. Maybe I should just throw out my dictionary and save myself tons of work in writing.

Lastly, we have the topic of spirituality. Obviously, the words "spirit" and "spiritual" are inclusive in "spirituality".

According to the first three out of four definitions provided by my edition of Webster's Dictionary, spirituality refers to the clergy, church-related matters and religious values. Breath or animating life are not inclusive definitions for "spirituality". Although which church was not specified, presumably it is the Christian church.

What about believers of the other faiths? Would spirituality be off limits or would it exclude them because they are not of the Christian faith?

We know for a fact that many students of eastern religions are in pursuit of spirituality.

Spirituality ought to name the study of spirit, rather than the study of ecclesiastical matters, soul, psyche or mind, per se.

Is spirituality like reality?

But instead of the physically concrete things that we can feel, touch and wrap our arms around, spirituality addresses the *real* things of the spiritual world that we can neither feel nor touch or wrap our arms around?

Could it be that, like the players in a game of house of cards, we are afraid to disturb the ivory tower lest the precarious tower smashes into millions of little pieces? Who would have the honor of gluing them back into one cohesive whole—the church, spirit, soul, psyche or our minds?

Spiritual inquiries matter.

Confusion in language must correspond to an overall confusion in culture.

In this case, the culture would be our own.

No wonder we have a crisis of Spirit.

What conclusion can we expect to draw?

In my humble view, the matter of our spirits and souls is too important to be left to chance, mere speculation or incestuous genealogy.

Chapter 6.

Multiple Angles

Supposing you are an alien who accidentally landed on Earth. In the galaxy system where you are from, an exchange of value is not symbolically made by the exchange of money. Therefore, you have never seen a coin. You do not know what a penny, nickel, dime, quarter or silver dollar represent.

One of the reasons you are traveling from galaxy to galaxy is because you are an esteemed anthropologist. Where you are from, they call you U2-Bleep-Bleep-384—or U2-384 to your friends.

You have been assigned the task of exploring the universe. Your role in this task is to provide a comprehensive record of the novelties you observe. In the region of the universe where you are from, record keeping is the most valuable commodity.

Here on Earth, you come upon these strange, small round objects. You watch the native inhabitants hand different groupings of them to each other—back and forth. You also watch them pick up a random array of, what appears to be, usable goods in conjunction with the back-and-forth exchange of these round objects.

You sample a few of them. Your analysis shows that they are made of metal alloys. You observe that they are not edible. You observe that they do not appear to keep anyone warm. You observe that they do not generate any energy and therefore are not a suitable resource of combustible fuel.

You are quite puzzles by them. If they are not a source of

food, warmth or energy, then of what value are they to basic survival, you wonder?

You decide to take a closer look. You see that the image on one side appears different than the other. You hold them in your "hand". You note that they make rather good flying objects. "Ah, a sort of small flying disc," you say with fondness. You are also able to stand them on their side. However, in this position, they do not seem very stable, because they fall over easily.

When you broaden your exploration of this new planet, you discover that everywhere you go, these round metallic objects are present. Not only that, everyone seems to be passing them back and forth amongst each other.

You find the whole thing a bit strange and mysterious. You have never encountered anything like this in all your other space travels.

You draw the following conclusions from your observations. Using what is familiar to you from your own region of the universe, you conclude that the round objects must represent a crude rendition of microprocessing information recorders.

You equate their flatness with an utility you are familiar with in your world—that of a historical record-keeping journal. Recording journals are quite flat where you come from. The flatter and thinner they are, they more records they can store. In your world, your have discovered how to get the most out of condensing everything.

You equate one of the flat sides with the images of a figure's head, some writing and numbers with time.

You equate space with the other flat side that features the image of an eagle or buildings.

You equate the entire object with what would be comparable to a multi-tasking silicon microprocessor. Why else would time, space and history storage be incorporated into one single object and passed back and forth amongst its denizens?

Now, replace the coin with Spirit.

As with the coin analogy, Spirit presents multiple facets.

However, whereas the coin displays three physical angles of view, Spirit could be represented, conceivably, by triple-digits of multiple angles—most of which are nonphysical.

From Spirit's vantage point, time, for example, is viewed from one angle; space from another angle; volume and density might be condensed to the extent that shrinking and compressing actually magnifies an effect; telescopic and microscopic-viewing lenses are synonymous; and its mysterious answers for the game of life are stored in sophisticated historical microprocessors as condensed obscure codes.

If Spirit could talk, what would it say?

What would its voice sound like? Would it have a confident, commanding, weak or tentative voice? Would it roar its opinions or would it diplomatically concede its vocal platform to some other aspect of the person, such as the personality or ego perhaps?

What would Spirit tell us about life or its ideas on life?

What would Spirit tell us about its thoughts regarding why it cohabits a physical form?

Based on his observations of humanity, what would an outer space visitor discern about our various versions of spirituality?

A shift in views regarding these basic premises of our ordinary physical reality creates a perceptual shift in our ordinary capacity to view all aspects of Spirit in a given moment of earth's time.

As U2-384 is with his coins, Spirit's many facets may appear quite perplexing to us. When in actuality, the mystery may be as simple as knowing what a coin is.

We just haven't arrived at a stage in our evolutionary development where we can view all of the pieces in one glance.

In this paradox lies the mystery.

Chapter 7.

Literal Data / Mythic Metaphors

When it comes to spiritual mysteries, part of the mystique stems from confusing concrete data with subjective interpretations, and vice versa.

In life, objective data *literally* helps us to verify that concrete events actually happened.

On the other hand, the exquisite words of poets and muses are more suited for their metaphoric embellishment of mystifying phenomena.

We can state the following:

Spirit does not *literally* manifest in physical form.

An exploration into Spirit cannot be *literally*—meaning factually—verified.

Therefore, it is inadvisable to get too caught up gathering formal data.

As such, any substantive discussion is open to liberal interpretations.

Although these characteristics may be inherently predetermined by the mystery, Spirit is not a metaphor.

Spirit *literally* animates us with life.

The heart, for example, is literally an organ of the body. Its physiological job is to pump oxygen-rich blood. Its design uniquely and successfully serves this purpose. The heart is literally a large mass of powerful tensile muscles operated by one of nature's most precise timing mechanisms.

The heart is also a poetic organ. Cardiothoracic surgeons who open up the chest cavity will not read epic poems of human triumphs and tragedies written by the physical heart. Yet, the poetic function of the heart is a widely accepted, universal and indisputable truth among our kind.

"High spirited", for example, does not literally infer that Spirit is a fifty-foot giant or that a person is inebriated with spirits.

"Giving voice" does not literally mean that a book can literally speak for its author or vocal cords are literally grafted onto groups of disenfranchised people, victims of abuse or preverbal children.

Few readers would read "game" in the title of the book literally, because this book is obviously not about hunting exotic animals, shooting pool or solving a crossword puzzle. On the other hand, does "life" in the title literally stand for survival, as in life and death, or is its reference philosophical?

Can spiritual mysteries be both literal and metaphoric, or neither?

Because that is not the point.

The main point of spiritual explorations is to know the forest from the trees.

Our capacity to discern subtle distinctions can cause spiritual mysteries to be even more shrouded; or, it can create a domino effect in our unveiling of them. "Domino", in this context, is a metaphor. It does not literally equate the "game" of life with the game of dominos nor does dominos have anything directly to do with Spirit or our realizing our purpose in life.

Are we prone to mixing our literal intents with our poetic metaphors, or vice versa? How would a third party discern a difference in their intended meanings? Would our ability to decipher between literal data and mythic metaphors help unravel spiritual mysteries?

Let it be clearly stated that in the four volumes of this series, Spirit does not literally stand for God in the Christian Scientist sense or a disembodied entity in the occult sense.

Although our language can either clarify or mess us up, what recourse do we have but to give it our best shot? "Best" and "shot" do not literally stand for "taking aim and shooting someone dead."

When it comes to *spiritual* language, some poetic license must be granted.

In spiritual exploration, where language is concerned, we must carefully ride a fine line between our literal and metaphoric intents. Although life is not literally a game, such as rugby, poker or chess, it is very much like a "game" in that there are players, rules, strategies and differing versions and interpretations of the game.

The fact is: we cannot literally beckon Spirit and soul to stand before us and have them verbally answer our haunting questions.

Besides, where its communications and expressions are concerned, Spirit may be more adept at using telepathic means than human language.

How literally or metaphorically should the previous sentence be interpreted?

If a simple object such as a coin can literally take on multiple angles, exploring the soul of humanity must be allowed some poetic latitude as well.

Whatever the answer, we must not let spiritual metaphors seduce us.

By the same token, we cannot expect to clarify spiritual mysteries by taking everything we think, know, read, see and hear too literally.

Stage 2.

Common Denominators

Act 2.

Guardians of Harmony

Quiet. Invisible. Yet strong.

Chapter 8.

Substantive or Decorative

Eskimos have more than a dozen words for snow. Powder, slush, icicle, sleet, hale, compacted and melting snow represent different forms of frozen water that falls from the sky and aggregate on the ground. Eskimos need many words for snow because their existence depends on their ability to accurately describe the frigid conditions of their harsh environment.

In western society, we have many different words for money: bills, coins, bank notes, certificates of deposit, credit, loans, assets, trusts, financial instruments and dough. For us, our existence seems to be dependent on our ability to accurately describe our financial conditions.

There are many other examples. Bread, pasta, semolina, macaroni, spaghetti and crust are different kinds of edible flour. Foundation, rouge, lipstick, mascara and eye shadow are different types of makeup.

I pose a very simple question.

How is it that we have a multitude of words for the common things in life, yet when it comes to naming that magnificent force of nature which gives us life, our articulations and dictions fail us?

We ought to have a few more words and descriptions besides spirit and soul.

How are they different?

Are they the same?

How do we describe their differences or similarities?

Is it spirit, soul, mind, heart or psyche?

Do we mean to say spirit, soul, mind, heart or psyche?

How do we compare notes?

How do we know if we are each speaking about the same thing?

Why is it important?

Is the issue at least as important as words for snow, edible wheat or makeup?

If in our language, we do not make distinctions regarding the different facets of this mysterious force which animates us with life, what does that say about what we truly value in being alive?

Would this force, at the very least, present with more diversity than snow, bread or cosmetics

If so, how much more?

Ten-fold? Fifty-fold? Hundred-fold? Or much more?

Would this force, at the very least, rival planets, stars, asteroids and nebulae?

Where are the words to match its breadth and expanse?

If every discipline of study begins with a common ground of basic terminologies, their definitions and conceptual framework, why is it then that, when it comes to the topic of spirituality, our systematic inquiries, in my humble opinion, fall drastically short of the mark?

These observations are not judgments. They are simply statements of facts.

Who are we afraid to offend?

What do we imagine would be the consequences of our offense?

Or is it that our heads are stuck in a celestial wormhole to the extent that we forgot how to turn inward and be intimate with our spiritual nature?

Would this force take offense if we did so?

What would become of us if we genuinely connect with

life so intimately that there is no doubt in our hearts, minds and psyches?

I dare to ask a very simple question.

"What are we talking about?"

Chapter 9.

Spirit: "Lifeline"

An intangible, yet magical, energy *forces* life into us. Without it none of us would be alive.

In this series of four volumes, Spirit is defined as "the energy force that animates us with life."

Spirit is the animating being.

Animating means, "energizing".

Without our capacity to pinpoint the exact mechanism of how it animates life, suffice it to say that, Spirit acts as an *intricate relay system* between the soul and self.

We can simply call this essential and vital connection a lifeline. Think of it as a sort of intermediary conduit, channel or bridge.

How it does this is one the greatest mysteries of all times.

This lifeline induces an individual and unique connection from each soul to the self.

The contact is not visible to our naked eyes or ordinary senses.

When this contact is intimate, we "get" life. When this contact is weak, the person lives without solid anchors to those life values that are truly important.

People who are spiritually directed are full of energy. They exude passion and enthusiasm. They seem to have a natural abundance of drive in life without having to work hard for it. Their animating presence infects us with their exuberance. We feel as uplifted and high on life as they are.

For now, the image of a child's hand holding a balloon by its string helps to crudely illustrate this contact: Spirit is (metaphorically, not literally) represented by the string. The hand (literally and metaphorically) represents the person. The inflated balloon metaphorically (not literally) represents the source of Spirit's animating energy force—which will be discussed in the next chapter.

Spirit lives with and through us.

After our physical bodies give out, Spirit lives on.

Spirit can and will exist without a physical host.

As such, Spirit is a bit of an adventurer. Just as Homer's epic poems recounted the long wanderings of Odysseus in the Odyssey, Spirit might be likened to a life player who ventures outside the region where the life team is stationed. Like the alien anthropologist, to travel, wander and explore new "frontiers" may be one of Spirit's missions. It may be the player who experiences many different life forms and gathers information about everything outside its native region where it has roots. It might even be the player who pillages and sows its wild seeds (whatever that might be for a spirit).

Eventually, all wanderers must return home, fuel up, recuperate and share what they have observed and learned about the strange new worlds outside its native region. Then, being the ever-adventurous sojourner, it wanders again.

When might Spirit stay put?

Perhaps when it has run out of adventures, adventurous places to visit and/or adventurous life forms to meet. Or, through its many successful adventures, it earns permanent recognition as a source for life's animating energy force (see next chapter).

The life-giving tasks performed by Spirit are substantive and vital to our survival. None of us could be alive without Spirit.

Again, life is synonymous with Spirit and Spirit is synonymous with life.

These statements are about as conclusive as we can expect to be when we use our crude words to describe Spirit's mysterious ways.

In every instance in this book, Spirit refers to "your" spirit.

Chapter 10.

Soul: "Source"

Soul is ageless, timeless and limitless.

In these four volumes, soul is defined as the eternal being.

Eternal means, "ever lasting, forever, extending to infinity and beyond the scope of ordinary spacetime."

Soul is unchanging and unchangeable. It is the eternal and unchanging quality we feel in the depth of our "soul" (being).

We often equate essence with soul.

Soul is essence, because it is the source.

Just as an ordinary garden sprinkler continuously emits a gentle cascade of water, source refers to the primordial outpouring of soul's fountainhead for life's energy force.

Soul is Spirit's source of energy. Soul is, therefore, also the source point for the essential self.

Because soul is the originating outflow of lifeline energy for a human being, it is the invisible power influencing the development of Spirit and its human vessel.

Soul simultaneously percolates in the deepest reaches of each of our being and pervades a mysterious nonphysical dimension beyond the known cosmos, of which the inadequacies of our language can barely articulate and describe.

Soul is everywhere and nowhere.

Soul exists outside of time and space.

A connection to soul is essential and vital for every human

who lives and dies.

Think of the soul as a supreme guide and reference for Spirit and essential self.

Soul's profound influence is everlasting, regardless of whether the person does or does not consciously makes a connection with the soul during his/her lifetime.

Furthermore, irrespective of the person's religious, non-religious, spiritual or non-spiritual inclination, the connection remains intact and incontrovertible—making this connection universal in the playing field of life. One reason that Christianity does not name a Holy Soul might be because soul is, by its very essence and definition, sacred and holy.

The essence of the soul is so basic, essential and vital to human survival; we cannot do without it—not by even the teeny-weeniest drop.

As we go about living our busy lives, many of us tend to forget that soul is the ultimate and permanent existential element of the utmost importance.

Soul does not forget. Soul "gets" it. Soul is the primordial animating source stretching beyond the physical plane of our ordinary existence or rational knowledge. That is why our soul is our essence.

If soul could speak, in its wisdom, it might say to us:
"How could you, humanity, get me mixed up with spirit?
How can spirit and I and be exactly the same thing?
Two of the most important and essential features
of human life, cannot and should not be represented
by such careless and sloppy use of language!
This may be the root to your existential problems.
No wonder many of you seem to have a hard time
figuring out 'the mystery'?
Perhaps you should come to a consensus
amongst yourselves over 'which is which'.
It may expeditiously solve the dilemmas
many of you create with your inability to precisely

articulate what it is you mean—soul or spirit—
of which humanity's histories have chronicled
too many bloody crusades, inquisitions and religious wars."

Although we tend to use "soul" and "spirit" interchangeably in our casual conversations, even in our everyday uses of these two words, we do make the subtlest of distinctions.

In the depth of our hearts, we are eternally connected to soul. For example, in the beautiful ballad by Rod Stewart, he croons: "you are my lover; you're my best friend; you're in my soul"—and not "you're in my 'spirit'".

Colloquially, soul is often used to mean "person", as in "lost soul" (rather than lost spirit). It also implies depth, heart and core, as in "body and soul" (rather than body and spirit). When we say, deep in our core, we mean deep in our "souls" (rather than deep in our "spirits").

Spirit, however, denotes zeal, zest or a joie de vivre (passion) for life. Spirit implies an effervescence or exuberant bubbling over with the vitality of life's animation. For example, we say: team, company, championship or holiday spirit (rather than team, company, championship or holiday "soul").

Just as the poetic heart is a symbolic reference, in science, soul is often used to allude to the mind. Dr. Valerie Hunt titled her book on the science of human consciousness, *Infinite Mind*, which, going by the book's strong emphasis on mystical truth, could have just as well stood for Infinite Soul.

Doctors commonly speak of the soul as the "life energy" of a body. For example, Dr. Christine Northrup, a holistic gynecologist, on an episode of Oprah, spoke of the soul (rather than spirit) leaving the dying body and a physical shell remains behind. Dr. John Upledger, inventor of CranioSacral Therapy and one of my mentors, confused the heck out of me during a workshop demonstration with his inference that my mother and I originate from (as in, sharing) the same spirit. He made it a big point that he did not mean soul. One would assume that doctors ought to know the name for the animating energy that sustains or exits the body, since we entrust them to navigate the course of life and death as part of their job.

In your world view, which is it that leaves the physical body at the time of death? Is it the soul or is it the spirit?

Not sure?

More confused than ever?

What we know very conclusively is that the soul does not take material form and cannot be seen by the naked eye; yet it is very real.

In my world view, at the time of death, the Spirit splits off from the physical host and rejoins the soul.

Chapter 11.

Self: "Whole"

Without exception, every human being is endowed with a self.

Self is "who you are".

In these four volumes, self refers to the essential being.

To reiterate, essential means "basic, fundamental and indispensable."

Think of the self as the "host" who contains and houses the life force energy (Spirit) that keeps us alive.

The self is the entire and complete warehouse of a person's biographical experiences up to the present moment in time.

The self is a composite of the physical, emotional, mental, psychic and spiritual aspects of an individual.

The self is greater than the sum of all its parts.

The self is the vehicle through which Spirit and soul mediate their wills.

Throughout the duration of a person's life, the self remains whole, intact and complete.

The self is whole because it is born complete

The self is intact because, regardless of the circumstances and events that shape a person in life—whether they are heroic, tragic or triumphant, the essential self cannot be broken, split or ripped apart. The presence of the essential self will always remain intact during the course of a person's life.

The self shows up buck naked for every one of life's events, irrespective of the seriousness or ordinariness of the affair. More about how we outfit ourselves in a later chapter.

In the game of life, the essential self must be in charge of and responsible for directing all other parts of itself.

Using the game of baseball as an analogy, the self is the life player who must always stand firmly on home plate. The team dynamic is such that the self holds the most important position on the team. Think of the self as the source point around which all other life players revolve. The self is the central pivot around which all dramas of life are enacted.

The essential self does not ever leave home plate.

From "home plate", the self directs all of the other players.

Without the self, the rest of the players in the game of life would be obsolete.

Although the influences of the self may be "hidden" from view, the essential self always remains present.

A "self" does not take material form and cannot be seen by the naked eye; yet it is very real.

If these descriptions seem obvious and self-evident, then why is it that very few of us live by this truth?

That the adjectives, "intact", "whole" and "essential", are needed to qualify what "self" stands for signifies a fragmentation of our essential being. Such an existential crisis seems to plague modern man.

The will to heal a division in the essential self is a driving motivation for exploring Spirit. (A division does not infer a split but rather a disconnect, disjointedness and/or disharmony amongst the players of the life team.)

The triad of self-spirit-and-soul is incontrovertible and ubiquitous. They must maintain an intimate contact at all times, because they form the foundation out of which the rest of the life players can have existence.

Chapter 12 .

Connection

All of us make connections of one sort or another in life.

We certainly hear it talked about a lot these days.

The issue is not whether we are or are not connected.

The problem stems from not connecting intimately.

To be intimate is to be so closely meshed that not one nanometer, micron or Plank's constant separates Spirit and soul from self.

Intimacy implies that an invisible, day-glow neon sign continuously flashes its messages: "Private Property, No Trespassing, Trespassers Beware", for all outsiders to take heed.

An intimate connection is not made with the ego.

An intimate connection is not made with the personality.

An intimate connection is not made with the superego or id.

An intimate connection is not made with the psychic network channel.

An intimate connection *is* made between self, Spirit and soul.

Spirit acts as the spiritual messenger (lifeline).

Soul acts as the sender of spiritual messages (source).

Self acts as the physical host for both Spirit and soul (connection).

An intimacy between self-spirit-soul spontaneously connects us with grace.

An intimacy between self-spirit-soul spontaneously connects us with passion.

An intimacy between self-spirit-soul spontaneously connects us with creativity.

An intimacy between self-spirit-soul spontaneously connects us with peace, calmness, a quiet confidence and our dreams.

An intimacy between self-spirit-soul spontaneously connects us to our real purpose in life.

Last but not least, such an intimate connection spontaneously connects us with god.

We do not doubt.

Act 3.

All in the Family

Good teamwork requires

Collaboration

Coordination

Communication

Integration.

Chapter 13.

Ego: "Avenger"

If ego and the triad of self-spirit-soul were to face off as dueling gladiators in the ageless amphitheater of life, fighting to the death to recover an authentic claim over the individual, who would undoubtedly win each and every time?

There would not even be a show down. Self, Spirit and soul will *always* rock.

To jump from the dynamic trio to ego may require a huge leap of faith—as far as ego is concerned.

In spiritual conquests, comic strip super heroes valiantly parody ego's role in the life team. As Superman, Batman and the Incredible Hulk are to the world of Captain Marvel, ego perceives itself as the avenger of truth, justice and righteousness in the world.

Strictly speaking, ego is the part of the essential self who uniquely performs the function of factually checking reality. That is: when there is cooperation and communication among all team members.

Although ego is an intrinsic and universal life player within every human being, existential fractures within the life team causes the ego to become a defender over *all* matters of life.

Unfortunately, a defender cannot perform reality-checking functions well because it cannot be counted on to be consistently factual and accurate. Hence rather than helping to inflate the self with life-enhancing energies, the ego turns into a grossly exaggerated superhuman.

What does ego have to do with Spirit?

Spirit must appear intangible and "unreal" to ego. After all, the primary function of an ego is to check the reality of the mundane, ordinary and factual sorts.

A defiant ego may, therefore, view Spirit as a nonentity. Spirit is not "real" in the sense that it is not made of physical matter. In its vigilance to maintain a semblance of ordinary factual reality, Spirit may appear to ego as a misplaced delusional apparition—much like a ghost.

To an overly defended ego—"who has gotten a big head for the wonderful job that it has been doing of running the entire life show"—anything not concretely material must be relegated to the category of inconsequential, nonsensical and imaginary. The paradox is that ego does not take material form and cannot be seen by the naked eye; yet it is very real.

Ego is infamous for causing trouble and headaches when one is striving to lead a spiritually purposeful life. In Hindu teachings, for example, ego is commonly banished for its propensity to wreak egotistical havoc in the self's virtuous pursuit of serene and mindful consciousness.

From ego's perspective, Spirit and the exploration of spiritual matters are superstitions based on the occult, magic and sorcery. Like ghosts, spiritual matters are neither here nor there.

In short, it "can't be bothered with it."

After all, the ego has more important matters to care for: such as making sure that the person stays alive at all costs. Nothing deters ego from its delusional perception of its paramount and important role in managing the life team.

If only poor ego would realize that without Spirit, it would not exist—let alone have its defensive job to perform.

The fact that Spirit must precede with its life-sustaining introduction before ego can be an avenger in life has completely escaped ego's well-defended "logic".

In its capacity to verify reality, ego might be willing to concede to the fact that: for it, instead of the essential self, to be on home plate is to permanently stall any hope of making spiritual progress. Yet, without an ego, we would make an even bigger mess of life.

Herein lies the dilemma in any spiritual exploration.

Many people gravitate to positions of social power because their egos are being amply rewarded. The ego demands a regular supply of stroking and is driven to realize its narcissistic quest. The quest is, however, not based on an intimate contact with Spirit. The quest is driven by an avenging ego.

Virtually every virgin ego will, therefore, initially defend and deny the existence of Spirit. Yet its defenses will cost the essential self and the rest of the life team access to Spirit.

Let it be clearly stated: ego is a subset of the psyche. The psyche is a subset of the human mind. (More about these attributes of the self in Act 4.) We cannot expect a subset of a subset of the total self to take command of a life.

To ride the precipitous fine edge so that ego is maintaining optimal balance between its reality checking capacities and overzealous defenses is one of the most challenging mysteries in the game of life.

When ego distorts the role that it is meant to serve to the extent that even its rightful owner cannot gain personal access to his/her self, inevitably the person will experience a crisis in spirit, at some time in life.

Chapter 14.

Superego: "Conformist"

Ego and superego love to tango.

The more passionate and intense the tango, the better the two are fed a regular diet of psychic turmoil.

However, ego, given its noble view of itself, must recoil at the implication that another team player is superior to it, at least in name. In ego's view, what could the role of a "superior" to ego be?

Superego is the super conscientious self.

Superego is the life player who is socialized to know right from wrong; do's from don'ts; should's from shouldn'ts; and ought's from ought not's.

In other words, it is the super conformist in all of us. Superego would have us obey all rules and laws to the letter. Follow social conventions. Do as we are told. It reminds us to dot our i's and cross our t's. Stay inside the line. Do not venture outside the box. At the sight of a policeman, respond by quivering internally with enormous guilt because no matter how removed we are to the crime, we must be at fault.

A well-developed superego is necessary to social order.

An over-vigilant superego becomes a socialized do-gooder. For example, when the first words out of a stranger's mouth is: "the sheriff issues citations to dog owners whose dogs are not on a leash" instead of "hello, how are you"? is a bizarrely skewed superego greeting. For socialized etiquettes to take precedence over living, such a mind-set must evoke an anxiety-ridden existence. To be so constantly uptight and inhibited must feel immobilizing.

Some of our greatest love stories, Romeo and Juliet, The Bridges of Madison County and Titanic, for example, capture the heart's struggle between love or superego demands, such as honor, duty and security.

Within the same person, ego and superego often rage a tumultuous inner battle. Ego wants to be right at all costs and it will defend its distorted perceptions to the end—of life. Superego is so concerned about conforming it would rather "save face" than create a public spectacle or dissent from popular opinion.

Since nothing can be superior to it, the ego must avenge its intrapsychic status by superseding superego. Superego will very skillfully ignore ego, because it is society's moral safe keeper. To get a sense of how they can dominate an internal conversation, short skits and role-playing featuring these life players are given in Chapters 33-38.

This intricate duel is forever vying for power over the individual. Confusion becomes the intrapsychic dialectic.

Spirit, unfortunately, gets caught in the crossfire.

Spirit's primary job is to animate us with life. In order for it to animate life well, Spirit requires all life players to unite behind the same existential platform.

Caught in the psychic crossfire, Spirit is required to act as an intermediary in a continuous inner battle, instead of fulfilling its life-sustaining liaisons between soul and self. Spirit does not take lightly its peacemaking position.

After a while, Spirit becomes fed up and decides that the quarrel must stop.

Its attempt to find peace within its human host may require Spirit to take drastic measures. There is no need to spell out the nitty-gritty details.

Get ego and superego to shush.

Connect with Spirit. And you will realize for yourself what

I mean.

If you are still clueless, the rest of this book and its three subsequent volumes will offer many helpful clues.

Remember: superego does not take material form and cannot be seen by the naked eye; yet it is very real.

Chapter 15 .

Personality: "Traits"

Show business broadcasts the message: having a winning personality is a shining mark of social accomplishment.

Gordon Allport, in his 1937 book, *Personality: A Psychological Interpretation*, writes: "Personality is one of the most abstract words in our language, and like any abstract word suffers from excessive use. Its connotative significance is very broad. Its denotative significance negligible. Scarcely any word is more versatile."

I define the personality as "a composite of our unique personal traits and temperaments."

In the game of life, the personality is a player of face value and the self is a player of inherent value.

The personality is not an individual's essential nature.

The personality is not the essential self.

The personality is not "who you are".

The personality is not a person's self-identity.

The personality is only a fragment of the total self.

The personality describes the most superficial layer of the self. Superficial in the sense that it is the outermost "psychological skin"—and not necessarily that the public self is shallow or phony.

Personality traits can be described by one-word adjectives. Like an exquisitely cut diamond, the self is a blend of so many different facets; volumes would be required to capture each person's true essence.

Roses, for example, come in many different colors, such as red, pink, yellow, orange, salmon, white and purple. The color of a rose is one of its many pleasing traits. We would not identify a rose only by its color. Furthermore, no two roses are exactly alike. Besides its color, the heritage, bouquet, hardiness and other distinctive features are the traits that define the essence of a rose.

A rose by any other name is still a rose. A self by any other name is still an intact and whole self.

Personality is to people as color, bouquet, heritage and hardiness are to roses.

Like the different colors of roses, people naturally possess different personal characteristics. Some are naturally charming, friendly, nice, likable, boy/girl-next-door, wholesome, pleasant, bubbly, funny, goofy, awkward, stiff or shy.

All of us don a variety of "outfits" for different social events. Casually lounging around the house on Sundays, we prefer schlepping around in our most comfortable sweat clothes. When we show up for work, we wear our matching suits, pressed shirts, formal slacks and shiny oxfords. When we are invited to a five-star gala ball, we dress up in our sequins, tuxes and finest bling-blings. When we go to Sunday service, we put on our Sunday bests. When we go to the gym, we tote around in our workout clothes. When we go on a rugged hike, we dress appropriately for the occasion. We would not inappropriately wear an outfit for the wrong social activity. Showing up at work wearing hiking clothes may lead to gross social misunderstanding.

With each outfit, we inadvertently put on different "personas" to suit the social circumstance.

With each persona, we seem to spontaneously acquire the body language, moods, expressions and demeanor to suit our social outfits.

All of us have had to "put on" personas in our lives. Like actors in a play, these caricatures help us navigate through the numerous different roles that we must all assume in life.

They are the "public images" we show to the outside world. In this way, they function as a sort of existential *filter* for the essential self. Acting as a protective screen, they keep private those aspects of the self that may not need, or want, to be put on public display or open to scrutiny. For example, instead of the essential self, whose presence is not mandatory, showing up at the PTA meetings, supermarket or the company softball game, the self can hide safely behind the screen of the personality filter.

These personas are adaptations made by and for the self. In this way, the personality literally helps to conserving vital life-force energy (Spirit).

For some, the personality functions as an existential camera lens. Instead of standing securely on home plate, the self hides behind the lens and directs life through the aid of a prism. The problem arises when, instead of simply operating as a visual enhancement aid, the "lens" becomes an indispensable existential crutch. Because in life, some people would be blind—literally and metaphorically—without their visual prismatic aid. Existential and spiritual blindness hinders survival.

This begs the question: If the personality shows up in life wearing different outfits, what outfit does the essential self wear?

Nothing.

Just as we would not mistake heads, tails and a coin's side view for its intrinsic value—as a token of monetary value—we would and should not mistake the outfits and roles that we take on in life for our true essence.

Over time, to confuse our essential being with the filter-lens, whose only functions is to present a partial view of the total self to and of the outside world, creates a spiritual block.

If we lived life relying exclusively on the personality filter-lens, our lives will inevitably mess up, because personas and personal traits can have no real claim over personal power.

The reason being: a personal trait or characteristic cannot be expected to make an authentic connection with Spirit.

In the modern era, the personality has become the biggest deterrent in a personal quest to realize a spiritually fulfilling life. Because in the long run, many of us may find it difficult to sift through the roles that we have "taken on" in life-as opposed to choosing our roles—to the extent that both self and Spirit become lost. (*Wings of Inspiration*, Volume II in this series, explores a recovery of these losses.)

Can you clearly "see" the difference between your various roles and personas, and who you truly are, or are you viewing "who you are" through a distortion lens?

Personalities *do* take material form and can be seen by the naked eye; yet they are *not* existentially real.

Chapter 16.

Observer: "Witness"

The observing action views an event and factually records it as a video camera would.

To observe and bear witness is to verify and acknowledge that an event factually occurred, regardless of the many possible eyewitness accounts of the same event by different observers. All parties unanimously agree that: "such and such factually happened and we can bear witness as described."

To say that the observing and witnessing self is an extremely important life player is an understatement.

Mastering the skill of "observing in present time" what is actually happening; doing so without input from preconceived ideas, beliefs and judgments; and consciously disengaging from our internally generated rebuttals, editorials and rumblings of mental noises is the single most important life skills to acquire, master and perfect.

We would do well to cultivate and refine it.

To do so requires practice—in life.

We learn through our observations.

Judges, doctors, psychologists, lawyers and scientists are examples of professions in which impartial observation is a required skill. Objectivity accompanies their exploratory process.

Factual information must be objectively assessed before mysteries can be solved—whether scientific, personal or spiritual.

Practice by stepping outside yourself. In other words, mentally "step away" from your physical body (metaphorically, not literally speaking).

Then, objectively take a look around at your life's circumstances.

How?

By knowing that: an observer is objective and a witness is impartial.

Objective is "the ability to factually record a life event without subjective input"—most likely, of the emotional sort.

Impartial implies "neutrality"—in other words, not favoring or taking sides.

The observing and witnessing self does not take sides.

It does not pass judgments.

It does not give long, lengthy explanations, discussions, justifications, excuses and/or reasons. This aspect of the self has the capacity to be detached and dispassionate.

Know that the act of making an observation is volitional and mindful. Meaning: a conscious decision must precede the act of making an observation, because otherwise the "looking" would simply be an instinctual reflex.

In some of us, our ability to observe and witness is more developed. In others, it is exceedingly lacking.

Meditation, for example, provides an excellent forum for the observing self to temporarily join the essential self on home plate. Those of us who are schooled in the daily practice of meditation become well acquainted with the part of themselves that acts as an observer. Meditation trains the meditator to consciously observe the innumerable cerebral noises which incessantly distract us.

Without a functional observing self in place, there may be a disinclination to progress very far in spiritual development.

In life as well as spiritual exploration, having this skill set and aptitude gives the spirit seeker an added advantage in assessing how well one is *really* getting on in life.

Because given that the observing self, ego, superego, self

and Spirit do not take material form; cannot be seen by the naked eye; and yet they are very real; how would verifiable objectivity in our accurate assessments of the stake that each life player has over our lives be discerned from delusional thinking?

The observing self is the team player who ensures that the ego, superego and personality are accountable to the self, Spirit and soul.

This aspect of the essential self bears witness to the fact that what is being observed is indeed authentic, accurate, real and truthful.

Authentic means genuine.

Accurate means, "free from error".

Real means, "not based on fantasies or delusions."

Truthful means honest.

The observing self maintains mental, emotional and psychic clarity so that the person can authentically live life to the fullest.

Those readers whose immediate response is to impatiently jump to the conclusion that an English lesson is being given rather than a discourse on Spirit are either under-utilizing or not observing the extent of their psychic turmoil.

Act 4 .

Energy Pathways

*Inextricably interwoven
for the sole purpose of life.*

Chapter 17.

An Elaborate Interweaving

We are not one-dimensional beings.
We do not exist in a void.
Every event in life is contextual.

Furthermore, the contexts are multi-layered and multi-faceted.

We would not, for example, dream of owning a receiving device, such as a radio or television set, with only one channel. If we did, it would indicate that we were either extremely poor. The environment was extremely remote and barren. Or, our equipment was broken or outdated. In most cases, we would chuck the equipment and purchase a new one. No one in his or her right mind would want to put up with a receiver that operated on only one channel.

The same can be said of human beings.

In life and in exploring the mysteries of Spirit, we *own* and must *operate* multiple channels of energy reception.

How *well* we handle life depends on a dynamic and complex interplay between the multiple energy channels through which we receive life's information.

Optimally, we would want to be proficient in using an *intricate blend* rather than relying exclusively on just one channel.

Each pathway helps us to tap into Spirit's mysteries ways.

Because our reception of Spirit, just as our reception of god, reaches us via different energy pathways.

Chapter 18.

Mental

The mental energy pathway leads Spirit directly to conscious thought.

A pathway is a conduit for relaying information—be it from the environment or within.

Humanity proudly proclaims the mental energy pathway as its crowning achievement. We congratulate and extol ourselves as god's "thinking" being.

Yet, how can we authentically empower ourselves when in our minds, the fine distinction between the energy force that gives us life and the energy source that sustains that force is not clearly delineated? How can we claim to "know" and be aware of the full extent of our spiritual nature when we ignore and/or consciously skip over a basic precept?

First of all, do not selectively block your cognition simply because the topic of energy pathway is being introduced.

In our ordinary and normal lives, few of us correlate our conscious thoughts with energy. The idea may not automatically fit in with our thinking. To many of us, our lifeforce energy appears mysteriously elusive; whereas we "know" our thoughts to be tangible because we trust that we can monitor our own thinking process.

These views require many of us to rethink things through.

If we experience little resistant accepting the factual data that the ego, superego and soul, for example, are not visible to the naked eye, do not manifest physical forms and yet are very real, then we should not let our preconditioned skepticism short circuit our mental receptivity now.

Obviously, the mental energy pathway does not take material form and cannot be seen by the naked eye; yet it is real.

Although the mental energy pathway is humanity's pride and joy, many of us play a mental game.

We create mental cages with invisible bars. We live our lives "as if" life was an idea.

Rather than really living life, we live a life in our thoughts.

We hold onto our mental prison of fixed ideas as if our lives depended on them.

This is a game in itself: A reflex (knee jerk) based on an idea (conditioning) turned into a belief (trigger) escalates into fear (emotion) and creates anxious responses (psychopathic complex).

We then acquire the idea that our anxiety must be a given in our lives because we decided to associate our self-identities with our anxious responses.

By not observing to see how actual life events match our past experiences *in the present moment*, our ideas become ingrained behavior patterns which subsequently take on the status of beliefs.

We *believe* our "life strategies" help us cope in life.

In reality, we falsely interpret and gauge our responses in life.

In life, observation must precede cognition. When cognition precedes observation, we are living in a mental reality that exists only in our heads and not in real life.

Take a moment. Breath. Re-read the last few passages.

Everywhere you find yourself holding your breath. Stop. Breath. Clear your head. Regroup. Observe your current-moment reaction. Has anything changed or are your thoughts and body responses *exactly* as was before?

Let us open our minds and really think about it: spiritual information must come through via the mental channel. How else would or could we make coherent sense of it? And furthermore, articulate the mysterious information in a lucid fashion to others?

Regardless of our pre-existing ideas about it, as one channel of life's energy reception, the mental pathway is not favored one way or another by Spirit.

Truth be told, our thoughts and ideas come and go as gracefully as a gentle breeze.

If we would only permit such an idea to be our guiding thought.

The state of a person's mental wellbeing is an accurate indicator of his/her spiritual connection in life.

In your mental reality, does thought follow energy or the other way around? Does energy follow thought?

Your answer determines the energetic consequences of your ideas.

Spirit has the correct and accurate answers to the above questions.

Is it even conceivable that in its infinite wisdom Spirit does not "know" what is really going on mentally with some of us?

Our thoughts must shape the very essence of our lifeforce energy, as well as profoundly influence the other energy pathways. Enough said about mind over matter.

Chapter 19.

Psychic

The psychic energy pathway leads Spirit directly to the psyche.

By definition, the psyche is our unconscious mind. Think of it as the alter ego of the conscious mind.

Instinctual drives (id), ego and superego comprise the three divisions of our psyche.

In our casual speaking, we talk about people who are "mentally" unstable. In actuality, we mean, they are psychically, as in psychologically, unstable.

The id, ego and superego do not have a physical substrate or correlate. We cannot touch or hold the psyche. The psychic energy pathway does not take material form and cannot be seen by the naked eye; yet it is very real.

Lots of people also seem to confuse their psychic energy pathway with the spiritual channel. They *deny* an intimate contact, rather than take time and find courage to be intimate with their psyches.

Psychic splits fracture the self. The effect of which gives rise to mental psychoses, emotional neuroses, spiritual crises and physical sepses.

In an effort to avoid psychic pain, rather than exploring their psychic energy pathway, they gravitate towards developing their egos and balancing their superegos by taking mental shortcuts. Their mental rationale is that a pursuit of spiritual growth seems so much more appealing and seductive than a disciplined, lifelong program of psychic face-offs.

Psyche's obscure etymology (as was pointed out in Chapter 5) may be a source of our conceptual, and therefore spiritual, confusion over the mutually coordinated functions of the psyche, conscious mind and Spirit.

To say that the psyche makes a good game of hide-and-seek seem like child's play is a gross understatement. As the heroic alter ego of all conscious thoughts, the psyche plays a coy game of shadowing boxing with the rational mind.

In this way, many of us perceive any sort of contact with psychic phenomena to be strangely mysterious.

Case in point: Much ado is made about psychics who act as psychic "channels" for mysterious messages from the beyond and other metaphysical regions of who knows where. Literally speaking, psychics "read into" the energy manifestations of the unconscious mind, rather than vocalize the true voices of the essential self, Spirit or soul.

Consider this: if Spirit were capable of animating us with life, why would it endow some of us with special receptivity and communication with the otherworld while refuse the same privileges to others of us? Are we not as deserving? Are we less alive? Are we retarded psychically and, therefore, spiritually? The psychopathic logic makes no common sense whatsoever.

There is nothing mysterious.

The psychic pathway is not granted to a select few.

This pathway is universally granted to all human life.

Avoiding a lifetime of repressed psychic energies will not awaken our spiritual awareness.

Avoiding it only serves to delay the inevitable: a coming to terms. Because over the course of our lives, each of us must honestly face the depth of our psychic pain.

Everyone has access to his/her psychic energy pathway: The journey begins with emotional honesty.

Chapter 20.

Emotional

The emotional energy pathway is a close cousin to the psychic energy channel.

Truth be told, the psyche murmurs our innermost secrets to us via our emotional feelings.

Our emotions are primal.

Our emotions are what make us uniquely human.

As such, they paradoxically contribute to both our greatest strengths and downfalls.

We acquire an inheritance of emotional immaturity from those who came before us. To the ancient peoples, our emotions may have stood in the way of our becoming civilized. The tools for systematically studying the inner workings of the unconscious mind were not uncovered until very recently. In this way, our ancestors collectively passed onto us a legacy of their emotional underdevelopment.

For this reason, in a vast majority of humanity, the emotional pathway is blocked. There are mothers who do not pass emotional knowledge to their daughters because they do not take ownership of emotional avoidance. There are fathers who would rather alienate, isolate or annihilate their sons than appear emotional.

Many of us who feel emotionally pained, desperate or blocked look to psychics, gurus and psychiatrists to unravel the mysteries of our lives, rather than simply accept our emotions and thereby feel them. We have been brainwashed to believe that "being emotional" makes us appear mentally weak.

Now, even in modern times, instead of dialing into our own emotional storehouse of psychic insights, we still find it difficult to navigate our way through the torrential tides of our messy emotions.

Given that our emotions do not take physical form, we can agree that they mysteriously manifest as invisible energies.

Shame is an emotion. Love is an emotion—as are anger, rage, hate, sadness, sorrow, disappointment, fear, passion and a whole slew of emotional colorations in between.

Our emotions are like the motions of the water's surface on a moonlit night. The surface could be so calm it resembles a shiny reflective mirror or it could be as choppy and turbulent as during a torrential rainstorm. Our emotions modulate and change.

Human emotions may be the defining characteristic that mystifies Spirit. This peculiarly human characteristic must fascinate and, on many occasions, irk and perplex Spirit.

Perhaps this is why Spirit is so willing to return time and time again to animate us with life forces; so that, humanity and Spirit together master and harness the power of human emotions.

Could it be that through our emotions Spirit is letting us know how we are really getting on with our lives?

When the emotional pathway is blocked, because it is either underdeveloped or immature, unfortunately, so is an authentic access to Spirit.

This angle is worth exploring.

Practice these simple steps each and every day:

Name your feelings.

Feel your feelings.

Acknowledge your feelings.

Honestly speak them to yourself and others by saying: "I feel (such and such emotion)."

The more you ride the torrents of your feelings, the more they will lessen and subside. This is the truth and not magic.

To culturally advance our spiritual exploration by fearlessly peering into the steamy caldron of emotions, instead of paying handsomely for someone else to handle our emotions for us, strengthens our human contact.

The state of a person's emotional openness is the most accurate indicator of his/her intimate contact with life, humanity and Spirit. Conversely, emotional immaturity—personal, cultural or spiritual—is a hindrance because it causes each of us to struggle in life.

The next time you feel anger, rage, passion, depression and any other emotions:

Rejoice that you are alive.

That you can feel.

That your Spirit is within you.

That you are being given very clear messages about your choices.

And that your emotional energy pathway is working hard to serve you spiritually.

Have no doubt. Our emotions are a stronghold for the psychic energy channel.

You are your own best psychic channel. This channel tirelessly serves you well to the end of your living days. Do not carelessly give away its keys.

All that is required is for you to honor your emotions. What you choose to do with your feelings is up to you.

Chapter 21.

Physical

In your view, how does your body fit within the context of your spiritual energy?

Multiple choices:

Answer number one: "I am clueless (and therefore I am a spiritual virgin)."

Number two: "The body is just a slab of raw meat (and therefore slapping it around is permissible)."

Number three: "I take my body for granted (and therefore I carelessly use and abuse it)."

Number four: "Who cares (and therefore I speak for everyone and no one)."

Number five: "God is taking care of everything (and therefore I don't have to.)"

Number six: "My body is constantly breaking down on me; it hurts too much; ask me another time (and therefore I would rather avoid the issue.)"

Number seven: "You mean there could be a cause-and-effect connection?"

In print, choices one through six may appear outrageously absurd. Yet have no doubt, they are actual views that many people have about the intricate relationship between their physical and spiritual health.

Let us start from ground zero (the clueless) and work our way up to choice number seven.

Step One: Some mysterious invisible "stuff" animates life. For a lack of a better word and without getting into a scientific discussion, we can loosely refer to the invisible "stuff" as energy. In other words, although the body may appear tangible and dense, it is an amazing assembly of "invisible" energies.

Very simply put, the body is a physical host for Spirit's animating energies. Without our bodies, we would be a spillover of chemical soup with no clear boundary. This may not faze Spirit; but it would be very disconcerting for us.

Step Two: The physical energy pathway leads Spirit directly to the body.

The physical body is the energy pathway we are most familiar with. When we look in the mirror, we see it. We can physically touch it. We have simple names for many of its parts. When we look at each other, we clearly see the person's physical features such as height, hair color, body built, carriage and posture.

Therefore, many of us are of the view that because we can see and touch the physical body, it appears more real to us than the other energy channels.

Step Three: Although the physical may be the pathway we are most familiar with, it is also the most underused and misunderstood with respect to the reception of spiritual information.

Step Four: As any good host, when Spirit and the body "embody" a close-knit relationship, the physical energy pathway functions at maximal capacity.

On the other hand, when Spirit is neglected or assumes a minority position, then the body will malfunction. Whether it is today or many years into the future; invariably, a spiritual disconnect will and must influence the physical body.

Step Five: Spirit is a mystery because we have not figured out what is the exact nature—biochemical, physiological, biological, neurological, bioelectrical—of this precious energy force that keeps us going.

Suffice it to say, our physical energy pathway is crucially dependent on Spirit. Spirit must intimately align, connect, mesh, contact and intersperse with the physical body. Otherwise, the body will and must suffer the consequences.

Step Six: The state of a person's health or ill health is the most accurate indicator of his/her intimate contact with Spirit, humanity and life.

Getting enough rest and sleep.

Eating healthful nutrients.

Hydrating with plenty of clean water.

Staying free of toxins and harmful chemicals.

Honestly feeling a wide range of human emotions.

And fearlessly expressing our feelings are some of the most basic ways that Spirit wants us to care for and honor the vital role our bodies play in the game of life.

A body that is dis- eased may be Spirit's mysterious way of alerting its human host that s/he has strayed off course. Shamefully, the person may be "talking" the spiritual psycho-babble-talk but not walking the walk.

Consider every ache, injury, accident, trauma, illness and crippling physical handicap as an opportunity to explore the elaborate interweaving and elegant grace of animating a life with Spirit.

Step Seven: The physical container of the body is the main channel through which Spirit communicates with the essential self.

(The themes presented in steps one through seven will be explored in depth in forthcoming *Basic Manuals for Life* "BMFL" books.)

"Insight" is inward seeing.

In order to authentically gain spiritual insight, one must be willing and able to "see" into the physical container of the body.

To Spirit, this process does not infer a bizarre form of microscopic vision nor are we peering into our innards as fortune-tellers would read tea leaves. (A propensity towards the literal demonstrates a disconnect between the mental, physical, emotional, psychic and spiritual channels of reception.)

Because, aside from the obvious fact that Spirit inspires every living body with the breath of life, without a body, our other energy states would be superfluous.

And although most of us lack the ability to "sense" energy, at some point in our lives, all of us must concede that to be spiritually insightful requires us to respect, care for and "listen" to our bodies.

Chapter 22 .

Spiritual

Human energy would not be what it is without spiritual energy. After all, what could Spirit be but energy.

As such, it is a very special type of energy.

The spiritual energy pathway leads Spirit directly to the heart.

The heart is animated with life. If it weren't for the steady drumming of the heart, our unrelenting eternal quest to find the purpose of life would be a non-issue.

The voice of Spirit and its mysteries speaks to and through our hearts.

When we open our hearts, the spiritual information we receive is: authentic, truthful, trustworthy, real, untainted, profound, unconventional and non-mechanical. The heart unabashedly opens itself to experiencing all of life's opulence and sensualities as well as its atrocities and tragedies.

To live life from the heart space is to be intimately connected with Spirit at all times, even during the most trying moments.

In order to heal the deep wounds of the heart, the spiritual pathway must be made accessible to the essential self. Yet, in order for the pathway to be open, the heart must claw through the gnawing feelings of the yet-to-be-healed pains.

When the heart is blocked because its wounds deeply hurt

the essential self; Spirit feels remorseful. However, until or unless the hurt is courageously confronted, the spiritual energy pathway will also be blocked. (This theme will be explored in more depth in the next three volumes.)

Matters of Spirit affect our personal heart space just as our heart pains affect Spirit.

Such a dilemma leaves Spirit with little or no access to the heart. Without access, spiritual recovery and healing cannot authentically take place because the solution will not really stick. This yo-yo dynamic creates a vicious feedback loop that can cycle endlessly without ever reaching peaceful resolution.

Sadly, such a paradox is so commonplace; it is a wonder it has not gained more media attention.

Dialogues of the heart, and therefore of Spirit, must authentically come from the depth of the self and soul.

No one could or should speak for another's heart—and Spirit.

The heart is home to home plate. Ideally, Spirit sits in crowning glory with the essential self as they preside over all aspects of the human being.

Spirit is a mystery because its energy does not take material form and cannot be seen by the naked eye; yet it is very real.

From our heart space, Spirit's mysteries delight and engage rather than perplex or confuse us.

When we live from our hearts, we extend a welcoming invitation to Spirit.

We feel reverence for and are inspired by life. We find truth, beauty, peace, joy and Spirit in our hearts.

What we feel in our hearts is more real than what can be described using language.

Healing the spiritual energy pathway can have a profound effect on ailments of the physical body, conscious mind and unconscious psyche. This profound truth may never acquire enough factual, scientific, and/or research data to satisfy those of us who are cynical at heart because the mental energy pathway is humanity's main deterrent in intimately knowing Spirit.

By fearlessly opening our hearts and minds, Spirit's mysteries will spontaneously reveal their exquisite beauty to us.

Chapter 23 .

Existential

The existential energy pathway is not merely the brainchild of famed French philosopher Jean-Paul Sartre.

"Existential" is literally the energy pathway of living a life.

It is the sum total of all of the energy pathways described above.

In existence, all energy pathways must be integrated in order for the game of life to be played with pleasure, enjoyment, zest and, last but not least, played well.

Let us be candid and admit that in living life:

There are people who are intellectual geniuses; yet who are incredibly retarded at the University of Life.

There are trophy-toting athletes who wow us with their physical prowess; yet who are glorified thugs, thieves and lowlife criminals.

There are people who are very emotional and emotive; yet who constantly break down because they do not have the existential savvy to handle life's many ups-and-downs.

There are people who seemingly are gifted psychics. For example, they claim to receive communications from beyond; yet who are so ungrounded in the simple everyday that they rely on a cocktail of anti-psychotic and painkilling pills to get them through the day.

We have all met people who claim to be extremely spiritual but who are so poor at handling money. In their lives, they have no reliable way of feeding the kids, are destitute and always seem to be in debt (literally and metaphorically) because they mentally associate wealth with decadence.

We can safely assume that, for these people, the different members of the life team are not at the same stages of existential development.

A burning desire to be spiritually blessed will not manifest the wish in reality, life or Spirit for those who delude themselves into believing: they are existentially "on their way" just because they think it is so.

In this way, the mental and psychic energy pathways are again the biggest hindrance to the existential pathway and our living life to the fullest.

The point being: not only must there be equal interdependence among the players of the life team, there must also be an elaborate interweaving of all of the energy pathways.

Act 5.

Natural Order

*Stages in development and
life as a theatrical stage.*

Chapter 24 .

Growth

The miracle of human life begins as the sperm makes an explosive entrance into the ovum.

Nature performs its special brand of magic.

After nine months, when all things go well, we are born into the world.

We drink, gurgle and crawl our way into early childhood.

We practice standing, walking and then running.

We learn to control our bladders and speak our words rather than use our fists.

We go to school.

We learn to make friends.

We get jobs and earn our keeps.

If we are lucky, we get to go to college.

We find one very special friend that we promise to spend the rest of our lives with.

We make replicas of ourselves.

And the growth cycles begins all over again.

Is this all there is to a life?

Every animal on the planet undergoes similar cycles of growth in life. In many respects, animals "do" life better than us because they are not self-conscious and do not over-think life as we do. So what makes us different than animals?

If we were to ask someone: "How far have you come along in your spiritual growth?"

What would be the response?

Are these questions so profoundly mysterious that specialized language, rituals and privileged dignitaries are required to decode their hidden secrets for us?

What is wrong with using commonplace concepts and simple words that we are already familiar with? Because, they are inherently what we already know in life.

Such a view is certainly worth exploring.

Chapter 25 .

Age

Before we are told to chant, hum or drone spiritual affirmations in pursuit of enlightenment, perhaps we ought to gauge the spiritual readiness of the person and match the spiritual information we provide with its age-appropriateness by asking:

"How old are you, ego?"
"How old are you, superego?"
"How old are you, personality?"
"How old are you, self?"
"How old are you, soul?"
"How old are you, Spirit?"

The observing self can be trusted to answer objectively and honestly.

In life, "age" is the number requested by the innumerable applications that all of us have had to fill out and which we dutifully fill in. Nearly every application asks about our age, because it is an important criterion. Our chronological age offers a general indication about age-appropriate expectations and behaviors.

The physical age of a person can be stated very matter-of-factly.

Age is chronological. Subtract the year we are we living in from the year a person was born. The resulting numeric value gives the person's age.

The aging process requires no thought from us. Its programs

are programmed in our DNA by nature. We all "know" how to age.

Besides that, natural order requires it of us, regardless of our cognizance or proficiency. As nature's animating force, Spirit takes residence within us, just as our biological programs are impregnated in the nuclear fabric of our cells.

Given that we correlate chronological age with physical growth, the same logic would hold for spiritual age and growth.

We have all met people whose emotional age does not match their chronological age. The same analogy can be made with respect to spiritual age.

Out of curiosity, when was the last time we asked someone: "What is your spiritual age?"

The same question might be asked directly of Spirit: "What is 'your' age?"

In the second instance, we would expect Spirit to give an answer. If Spirit, for example, could fill out a job application for spiritual employment, perhaps it would tell us, by its own standards and in comparison with other spirits, what its age is.

What would its answers tell us about Spirit's reasons for taking form as a human being?

To further complicate matters, how would Spirit give its answer, given that Spirit does not have direct access to our vocal cords?

If spiritual employment requires that certain very basic minimum standards be met: for example, for it to be free of denial and resistance, just as we would require a potential employee to be free of substance abuse. A Spirit who is two years old could not be expected to be "free of denial and resistance"—just as a two-year old child could not be expected to grasp the consequences of substance abuse.

What is so strange about Spirit being of an age?

Everything else in human existence seems quite dependent on it.

Besides, we are not literally asking for it to confirm its

answer as fact.

Remember, Spirit came to us here on the earthly plane from another world. Time and space operate quite differently there. It is, therefore, prudent to assume that spiritual time is not kept progressively as a relationship between the migrations of Earth with respect to the Sun. Spiritual age, therefore, ought not be converted using the clock time of 365 days to the year.

Although few of its animated hosts have asked to know Spirit's age or how long it has been playing the game of animation, this line of questioning is provocative enough to peak our curiosity.

To correlate "age" with Spirit as a basic common denominator demystifies the exploration. The angle is certainly worth exploring.

Once the question has been posed, patiently wait for the response. Do not be surprised or shocked.

Whatever answers we get back give us a more refined perspective on life.

Spiritual age does not take material form and cannot be seen by the naked eye; yet it is very real.

Chapter 26 .

Development

Development is growth through sequential and well-delineated life stages.

What response would we receive if we simply asked someone: "How far have you developed spiritually?"

For example, every human being naturally progresses through predetermined stages of development: in our life stages from birth, infancy, childhood, adolescence, adulthood and parenthood to old age. In our psychological stages: dependency, exploration, rebellion, sexual maturation, separation and individuation. In our mental stages: ignorance, education, discipline, understanding, intelligence, awareness and knowledge.

Just as with physical aging and growth, our spiritual development must follow an orderly progression under the guidance of nature's laws.

If this does not seem obvious, it might be because we have been brainwashed into believing that spiritual progress is a privilege that can only be attain by a select few. This view indicates that our observing selves have not developed sufficiently to take objective notice. And, we have not allowed ourselves to intimately connected with these innate forces which drive a spiritual connection.

What must be obvious is that just as emotional immaturity and mental incapacity can affect one's performance in life so can spiritual underdevelopment.

Spiritual development is a "given" in the game of life.

This development is both innate and volitional.

Innate, in that Spirit has direct access to the internal impulses which direct our every response in life.

Volitional because we have a choice.

The dynamic interplay between these two driving forces is a part of the allure of the mystery.

Developmental stages do not take material form and cannot be seen by the naked eye; yet they are very real.

The topic of spiritual development is more complex than spiritual age or growth.

In nature, development is instigated by an individual's exposure to stimuli and response.

Spiritual development must be governed by similar natural laws. Compassionate and love, for example, motivates spiritual development differently than prejudice and hate.

Many of these spiritually sensitive topics, as well as discussions using the terms and concepts presented in this introductory volume, will be expanded and put into practical context in the subsequent three titles of the series.

Chapter 27.

Maturity

Maturity, spiritual or otherwise, does not necessarily come with ripe old age.

Maturity is defined as "reaching the optimal and maximal potential allowable within the rules and boundaries set by nature."

Maturity arises through the culmination of growth and development.

Trust, humility, detachment, empathy, compassion, altruism, acceptance and empowerment indicate spiritual maturity.

With spiritual maturity, we have acquired the capacity to embrace life with detachment. We practice humility. We bring service to others without a loss of our essential selves. We wholeheartedly accept the consequences, judicious or injudicious, that life deals. And we embrace our destiny.

We arrive at spiritual resolution.

Resolution brings insight.

We do not need authority figures to inform us what might be true or untrue—regarding Spirit, its mysteries and our rightful place in existence.

We feel calm and at peace.

We know with conviction that god exists.

We are not angry with god.

We know with conviction that life is not out to punish us.

We are more able to handle challenges. We can engage in

competition without being mean or doing harm to others.

We understand that in life, certainty, idealism and perfection are illusions. We do not expend vast amount of energy ignoring, avoiding, deluding or cheating while playing on the big stage of life.

With spiritual maturity comes the resilience and agility to cope with the various games that life would have us play.

Ethics and morality are not matters that we struggle with.

We do to others as we would do to ourselves because such behavior in action and thought is a natural outflow of our spiritual maturity. And not because our conscience is too afraid or too inhibited to do anything else.

With maturity come sophistication and a broader world view.

Maturity does not, however, come automatically.

Expecting someone who is *emotionally* immature to be accountable and responsible is futile. Expecting someone who is *mentally* immature to be cognizant and intelligent is frustrating. Expecting someone who is *physically* immature to move heavy boulders and go on a long, extended journey—both literally and metaphorically—is imprudent and unreasonable.

Likewise, we would not expect someone who is spiritually immature to be graced with wisdom, compassion or true knowledge. In other words, knowing "how to live".

To be a full-grown mature adult who has not begun to explore Spirit is to be spiritually immature.

In our playing the game of life, there are consequences to being spiritually immature.

For the most part, although we can neither alter nor control nature's order of spiritual rhythms, directions and nourishments, we do have a resounding choice over our personal growth.

Personal growth promotes spiritual growth.

Spiritual growth promotes a well being of the essential self.

A well being of the self motivates spiritual maturity.

Nothing would please Spirit more than to see every one of us become spiritually mature.

As spiritually mature human beings, we realize the merit of repeated practice. Those of us who are immature will find repetitions puzzling, stupid and downright annoying.

Needless to say, maturity does not take material form and cannot be seen by the naked eye; yet it is very real.

Act 6.

Natural Inheritance

Hug a tree.

Chapter 28 .

Instincts

Too bad we cannot interview Spirit and ask: "How do you, Spirit, view human instincts?"

Does Spirit embrace them or does it consider instincts to be primitive and vile?

Is Spirit of the view that our instincts need to be severely controlled or dominated over?"

Spiritual teachings encourage us to rise above our base animal instincts.

One of the reasons instincts are considered base by most spiritual teachings to be base is because animals do not possess conscious reasoning. As such, in an effort to achieve this goal, a majority of spiritual explorations tend to subvert rather than include our instincts in their discussions.

We have come a long ways, however, in our understanding since then.

Divorcing Spirit from its instinctual origins mistakenly denies a foundational cornerstone of life itself.

Consider this vantage point: Very simply put, our animal instincts help us to survive. Our instincts help us to stay alive; survive; and basically, stick around.

We are, after all, part beast and part reason.

Our instincts are precognitive. We are not required to interrupt our cognitive thought processes in order to taste, smell, hear, see or sense hot and cold. Our senses require no conscious thought. Like the hard drive of a computer, our instincts are pre-programmed in us.

Without our instincts, our chronological aging, physical growth, mental development and existential maturation would stall, let alone our hope of unraveling spiritual mysteries.

Instincts do not take material form and cannot be seen by the naked eye; yet their effects are very real. Our instincts are a part of our inherent nature. One reason Spirit is encoded in our DNA is so we would manifest and fulfill our natural directives.

If Spirit were the energy force that animates life, why would it operate separately or in isolation from nature?

Consider the probability that, just as physical, psychological, emotional and cognitive development are under the guidance of our DNA, our spiritual development must be also.

Profound truths often manifest with great simplicity.

Spirit must, therefore, accept and welcome our instincts. For without instincts, how could Spirit animate life?

One of my main points of contention is, humanity's spiritual quest arises from our natural instincts. Spiritual intimacy is innate rather than a special gift handed to a privileged few.

Repression backed by denial does not bring true awareness.

Spiritual teachings that favor an absolution of human instincts because they are regarded as base and primal repress our innate aggression.

Those of you who may feel offended by this fact are cut off from an intimate contact with your human instincts.

In life, aggression serves a vital purpose: it helps us survive.

As much as some of us resists, we can neither ignore nor escape from the simplicity of the fact.

To live life driven by instincts might not be such a bad thing. After all tens of thousands of magnificent animal species grace the planet.

Spirit may feel compelled to add:

> "Do you really believe that dogs, cats, birds and
> butterflies are divorced from me simply because their

modes of verbal communication differ from humanity's?
What would a dolphin or an elephant, for example,
tell us about their intimate contact with Spirit?
If I, Spirit, am not aligned with your instincts,
then where might I be—given that instincts
are an essential component of all earthly life forms?"

Who is to say that our spiritual quest does not innately arise from our instinctual drives?

Perhaps the main reason Spirit continues to elude humanity is because our cultural, philosophical and religious imperatives would have us divorce our spiritual nature from instincts.

Spirit must not be as disillusioned or repulsed by instincts as many spiritually enlightened voices would have us believe.

This angle is worth exploring.

Chapter 29 .

Common Sense

There is the world of our senses. They allow us to taste, smell, hear, see and touch.

"Common" implies a shared commonality that is basic to our five ordinary senses.

This "commonality" allowed us to survive in our natural habitat eons before indoor plumbing, freeways and metropolises existed.

Logic and instincts, working in unison, balance and harmony, lead to common sense.

In life, the duo of instincts and common sense help us stay alive better than our intellect can. They facilitate our practical adaptations in life because the sense in knowing is not intellectual. It is instinctual.

Common sense is a close cousin to our gut instinct.

Common sense does not take material form and cannot be seen by the naked eye; yet it is very real.

A fact of distinction is that university degrees are not, and probably cannot be, granted for the study of common sense. "Common Sense 101" is not offered as an academic course work because it cannot be taught.

Just as our instincts-in particular, our gut instinct is not something that needs to be learned-common sense is inborn. It just seems to come along with our whole package.

And, it does not wear off with living.

Common sense helps us to be reasonable: to sense what is real and within "common" reason in life.

Learned knowledge we acquire from outside sources. Common sense we get from our intuition.

A sense of "knowing how to" comes along with that which is "common". People who repeatedly ask "how to" do something lack common sense. By the same token, people who lack common sense will not know they lack it.

Why? Because they do not have common sense.

When we meet people who lack common sense, this particular deficit in life quickly becomes obvious. Trying to talk some sense into someone who lacks common sense can be an ordeal. For common sense to be overshadowed by over-thinking, over-analysis and over-intellectualization is to be mentally crippled in life. Every single detail must be corroborated, substantiated and validated with facts, logic and/or reason. It is like reasoning with someone who is endowed with a diminished capacity to handle life easefully.

When common sense is fully functional, the person does not need to break everything in life into minute details.

Lacking common sense, effortless living becomes exceedingly difficult, if not impossible.

Common sense, apparently, is not all that common.

Common sense tells us:

"The answer does not lie within
reason, logic or the material realm.

Our hearts and guts have always known the authentic answers—to our every query, including spiritual mysteries."

When we are cut off from our instincts, we lack common sense because, in a sense, we are disconnected from nature. We lack an intimate contact with the mysterious life force which sustains life.

Common sense facilitates spiritual exploration because it connects us with our innate memory that, in our nature, we are blended with nature. This permits us to be reasonable—as opposed to outrageously fantastical or fanatical, especially where spiritual insights are concerned.

If you lack common sense, the first order of business is to admit this fact. Then, you will want to reconnect with nature.

Chapter 30.

Intelligence

Life requires human intelligence to be more than purely intellectual.

The game of life is a battle for survival. Life, therefore, requires us to apply what we learn and know to global spheres of influence, rather than hold them as abstract ideas and concepts.

We have all met people who are extremely intelligent. They are highly respected in their areas of professional expertise. They attended the best universities. Many esteemed titles and initials follow their names. Their academic and scholastic pedigrees are impeccable and impressive. They are decorated with many prestigious awards of recognition. They can recite facts and trivia at the drop of a hat, yet they lack an integrated capacity to handle life at its most intimate and spiritual level.

Consequently, their personal lives are a total mess. They are not on speaking terms with their children. They have not met their grandchildren. Their spouses engage in extramarital affairs because of feelings of emotional void stemming from continual absence and abandonment. Their intellectual achievements notwithstanding, these people lack social graces and would betray their best friends at the drop of a hat.

Learning from our life experiences is a sign of higher intelligence.

Existential intelligence is having the smarts to realize that nature imposes very specific order in life. One of which is that life's mystery cannot be solved by cerebral intelligence.

Intelligence is defined as "an optimal coordination between stimuli and response using *all* of life's energy pathways."

Intelligence is *choosing* what is smart and putting it into practice in life. Ignorance is willfully repeating old patterns without bothering to fact-find.

Spiritual intelligence does not come about because of learned knowledge.

As we advance the intelligence of our machines, whose sole purpose is to serve us, let us not forget to advance the intelligence of our spirits along with our minds.

Without intelligence about Spirit, the person is only partly human. S/he has not fulfilled one of our mandates for taking physical form: spiritual awareness.

If Spirit could speak, it might say:

"I, Spirit, came here from a far-away place.
I bring a special brand of force with me.
I breathe it into you so that you may have life.
Would I, therefore, not be highly intelligent?
Too many of you lack the sort of
existential intelligence to really 'get' me.
Your over-reliance on intellectual trivia may be
the biggest deterrent to solving the riddle:
'What is my purpose in life,
why am I here and why am I alive?'"

Chapter 31 .

Joyful Play

In nature, play serves a strategic purpose.

Animals learn to hunt, defend, nest, socialize and procreate through play. In the animal kingdom, those animals whose playing do not culminate in expert gaming skills inevitably die sooner than those who do. These skills ensure their survival.

Human beings are no exception.

Play is pleasurable. Pleasure effortlessly instills and encourages positive associations in life. Play appeals to our sense of pleasure rather than pain.

Play is naturally encoded in our DNA. Rarely must we teach our children how to play. As our children play, their expressions of joy are infectious and bring a beautiful smile to our faces.

As one of god's creatures, we learn to perfect our gaming skills through play as well.

Joyful play serves a strategic spiritual purpose.

Considered from Spirit's perspective, life may be a game it is required to play. Therefore, for Spirit to animate us with life, it would make all the sense for us to live life to the fullest.

A curious disposition, light heart, an inquisitive mind-set, wonder, adventure, laughter, goofiness, silliness, daydream, creativity, joie de vivre, joy, fun, contentment and time alone are valuable assets in any spiritual exploration.

They help us not get stuck in a rut.

We know with every vibrant and tingling pulse in our pores

that we are living life to the fullest.

Human beings who approach living too seriously have forgotten how to joyfully play.

When we forget to be playful in life, our bodies stiffen with osteoporosis. Our minds become rote. Our hearts harden. The breasts of women become calcified. Their wombs become barren.

We lose touch with our most basic instincts, common sense and intelligence.

"No pain, no gain" may be a lesson learned by masochists and those who have been conditioned to equate fulfillment in life with pain.

Playing the game of life does not mean we are play-acting our roles. We are not being indulgent. We are not frivolous or aimless.

If we get too caught up playing acting, we lose sight of our essential self. When this happens, Spirit may feel compelled to catch our undivided attention by giving us a good knock up the side of our heads.

This angle is worth exploring.

Of the many spiritual teachings, those views that encourage a healthy balance between seriously taking in our life lessons while at the same time remembering to play are favored by Spirit.

Maintaining a playful spirit in life ensures that we remain open in our attitudes.

Stage 3 .

Our Blurred Dialogues

Act 7.

Stayed Tuned

Been there. Done that.

Chapter 32 .

Drowning in a Flood of Words

Did you know that a pregnant silence can pack more drama and substance than a runaway monologue?

The simple principle: "don't just tell me; show me" carries spiritual weight.

As a culture, we talk too much and say little.

We sound like a bunch of squawking parrots set on autopilot, mimicking just about everything we can mimic. However, instead of "Polly want a cracker", we repeat the same run-on stories, explanations, rationalizations and excuses. Furthermore, we seem to love to talk about ourselves and, in particularly, our woes.

Just because we live in a disposable society which thrives on disposing vast quantities of material things, our words are not disposable.

Our excessive use of empty words does not fool Spirit.

When we talk a mile a minute and say nothing substantive, our spiritual barometer is set on automatic pilot.

When we operate on autopilot, the essential self is not present to steer the wheels of life.

Life is dynamic and ever changing.

To go against the natural forces of life and verbally go on automatic pilot sets us up for inevitable failure and unhappiness in life.

We lose our intimate contact with Spirit.

On the other hand, by its intimate contact with us, Spirit knows what is truly going on with each of us.

Spirit realizes we are masking our flood of tears with a flood of rhetoric and spiritual party lines.

Do not casually or carelessly dispose of your words by talking nonstop, without stopping—to listen to yourself.

More importantly, in the quiet of silence connect with Spirit.

Chapter 33 .

Cheating Life

The following skit is a composite of several actual case studies and does not represent a particular person.

Ego: I am dying. I have leukemia. The doctors are giving me three months.

Body: I've been feeling sick for years. Why did I not take better care of me?

Observing Self: Who am I talking to? No one in here is listening.

Mind: I am.

Spirit: You are kidding me, right?

Mind: What's that suppose to mean?

Heart: I suffer from many mental delusions.

Psyche: I ache and I have a headache.

Ego: Wait a minute. They diagnosed me with cancer of the blood. I'm not delusional.

Self: Everyone must be quiet. I want to hear from Spirit. I don't have much time left.

Personality: Did someone tell Shirley?

Ego: I took care of it.

Superego: Ego did the right thing.

Personality: Ego did an excellent job.

Observing Self: I was there and I thought ego cheated.

Self (a big lump in the throat): I really wanted to hold her one last time.

Superego: That's not possible.

Personality: I can't even say a proper good-bye to Shirley?

Ego: No. Wanda can't find out about Shirley after all these years.

Self: How did I handle it?

Observing Self: I told her over the phone.

Psyche: What? My headache is getting worse.

Heart: I want to cry.

Personality: I can't cry. I must put up a brave front for the family. After all, I am still the head of my household.

Spirit: After 82 years, you still don't get it, do you?

Personality: I look pretty good lying here in my hospital gown.

Heart: Be quiet. I've had enough of you, persona.

Self: I took a mistress, cheated on my wife, had two kids out of wedlock with Shirley and I was never around for my own kids.

Psyche: Whew, that was a big load off my chest.

Heart: A cheating heart will bleed to death from the guilt.

Observing Self: Yes, eighteen years of lies, decoys, out-of-town business trips, missed holidays and birthday parties nearly did me in.

Ego: I kept going pretty well.

Body: I am cheating again. My lies do not fool anyone. All of "us" coexist in here.

Mind: I can fix this. I can fix anything that I put my mind to. After all, I've made millions as a venture capitalist. This problem can't be that hard to fix.

Psyche: This matter is entirely out of my hands.

Heart starts to cry.

Personality: That feels much better. I can let my guard down a little.

Superego: Is it all right for a grown man to cry? People will not think I am weak.

Self: I have played by other people's rules for too long. Before I depart, I would like to be freed of my obligations.

Heart: Anything else?

Observing Self: I must set things right by Wanda and Shirley.

Ego: What am I talking about? How?

Spirit: Tell them the truth.

Psyche: Tell them the truth.

Self: Tell them the truth.

Common Sense: Tell them the truth.

Heart (sobbing uncontrollably now): Will my wonderful wife of fifty-four years and my incredibly stunning mistress of eighteen years forgive me?

Soul: Release thyself in all respects by coming clean. Don't bring all that baggage with you.

Ego: But I am an atheist. I don't believe in God or heaven.

Spirit: It is not necessary.

Self: I know. I have always known. I am not afraid. I know what happens next.

Spirit (sigh): My job is finally done. I thought I would never see the day.

Soul: Job well done.

Heart: Let me let go of my guilt.

Ego & Superego: Yes, we admit we cheated two innocent bystanders. We feel remorse. We feel sad.

Observing Self: Let me set the record straight so I am not cheating again.

Psyche: I feel like I am about three years old.

Body: I feel like I am about three hundred years old. No wonder I couldn't properly cleanse and maintain my blood.

Superego: I cheated my entire bloodline.

Emotions: I've been stunted since I was a baby.

Mind: I cheated on two women and all of my children.

Observing Self: I've finally grown up.

Body: I feel as if a huge boulder has lifted from my entire body.

Psyche: I am not achy any more. I feel so much better.

Self and Heart: I want to tell the whole world what just happened. Will they believe me or think I'm mad?

Spirit and Soul: They will believe you if you speak honestly. By the way, you will live a little longer than the doctors' prognosis. You will have two more years with your beloved.

Ego, Superego and Personality: Had we known this was what was expected of us, we would have conceded to it a long time ago.

Self: I promise myself to make good use of my time left.

Chapter 34.

Running Life

The following skit is a composite of several actual case studies and does not represent a particular person.

Ego: I'm training for the Boston Marathon.

Body: I need to slow down. I am running on bare.

Mind: Stop whining. I can do anything I set my mind to.

Psyche: I am on top of the world right now. Everyone is clamoring for a piece of me.

Superego: I have to keep going. I can't disappoint the people who helped me get this far.

Personality: My friends, colleagues and clients adore me.

Observing Self: Family was conveniently left out.

Ego: Don't bother me with trivia. I am still biologically viable.

Body: I doubt I know what I am talking about.

Mind: I am still fertile.

Psyche: A little denial never hurts.

Ego: The truth may set me back a few thousand dollars in psychiatry fees.

Heart: I feel so lonely.

Self: I really want to share my life with someone.

Ego: I'm a runaway bride. I've backed down at the altar twice.

Superego: It's very impolite to gloat about it.

Self: Brad was wonderful. He really loved me.

Psyche: He suffocated me.

Personality: There was such a strong attraction. We fell in love immediately. I don't understand what happened.

Observing Self: Those are excuses. I ran away because I was afraid.

Psyche: I keep running away from intimacy.

Self: I am not sure why.

Spirit: I know why.

Personality: Who care, as long as everyone adores me.

Observing Self: I don't think I knows who I am.

Superego: Of course, I do. I give 100% of myself in service of others.

Body: Yes, that's why I feel so run down. I am so tired. I can barely think straight.

Observing Self (whispers): Maybe I need to have my thyroid glands checked.

Ego: Who needs thyroids? I know everything there is to know about the thyroid.

Mind: Don't be so anxious.

Body: My hormones are all screwed up and I can't get a good night's sleep. I have insomnia.

Heart: I'm tired. Father broke my heart.

Spirit: Father's harshness shattered my personality.

Self: Father broke my spirit.

Psyche: I think I am developmentally delayed.

Ego: Hey, where did *that* come from? I'm still in charge in here, right?

Observing Self: I need to slow down.

Personality: I am just fine. Ask everyone who knows me. I am upbeat. I always put on my happy face regardless of how I really feel inside.

Psyche: I can't slow down. If I slowed down, I might feel my brokenness.

Mind: Living this lie is better than mentally disintegrating into a million little pieces.

Superego: That's too melodramatic.

Observing Self: I am being superficial.

Spirit: It's too noisy.

Body: What's going on? All of a sudden, it's like someone dimmed the lights and I can barely keep my eyes open.

Psyche: I had to intervene.

Observing Self: I was starting to remember I have a big empty hole in my heart.

Instincts: Psyche conked me out so I don't have to face the real pain.

Mind: I can't zone out right now. I'm in the middle of a big project at work.

Psyche: Too bad mind only has control over my cognitive functions.

Ego: I'm right. I'm always right.

Spirit: She is very scattered.

Body: Why was I not consulted? Nobody asks me. I end up baring the brunt of my psychopathologies. When I am flat on my back with a burnt out thyroid, maybe I will finally wake up and stop running away from my emotional pain.

Self: No wonder I'm always on the go. My running around is my pathetic way of coping with life.

Mind: Hey, now I understand. My anxieties are because I'm constantly running on overdrive, in every respect.

Ego: Is there hope?

Spirit: There is hope. I haven't lost a case, yet.

Chapter 35.

Resisting Resistance

The following skit is a composite of several actual case studies and does not represent a particular person.

Superego: I will marry her. It's the respectable thing to do.
Personality: What will everyone think?
Psyche: I'll handle it.
Self: I'm only seventeen. I have my whole life ahead of me.
Instincts: I should have had more self-control.
Mind: I don't know what came over me.
Ego: I resist change.
Superego: I must marry her and take care of her and the baby.
Mind: That's not what I had in mind for my future.
Ego: I resist change.
Personality: My dream is to be an actor like Tom Cruise.
Observing Self: I got the same girl pregnant twice.
Common Sense: Her mom made her get an abortion the first time.
Psyche: I feel no remorse.
Self: I may be numb.
Mind: I may be numb.
Psyche: I have always been numb.
Instincts: Am I numb, also?
Heart: I feel deeply.
Self: Two precious spirits.
Spirit: Correction. Three beautiful spirits, myself included.
Ego: I have no need for spirit. I resist change.
Instinct: That's dumb.

Mind: Arrogance.

Personality: I don't know how to change; however, I do know how to resist change.

Superego: Do the right thing.

Observing Self: I'm about to screw up my life, her life and the life of my baby.

Ego: It's always better to go out with a bang.

Common Sense: How immature.

Superego: Pompous ass.

Personality: What to expect? I'm only seventeen.

Mind: I'm using the age thing as a hedge against not having to change.

Observing Self: What's the resistance about?

Ego: Don't smother me with the pop psychology BS.

Common Sense: Like I said. How immature.

Heart: I'm scared.

Psyche: I feel overwhelmed.

Self: Maybe there's hope for me, yet.

Our resistance is futile.

When we deny Spirit, we deny life.

When we ignore Spirit, we ignore life.

When we are oblivious of Spirit, we are oblivious in life.

When we avoid Spirit, we avoid what really hurts in life.

When we reject Spirit, we reject life.

When we resist Spirit, we resist life.

Spirit may want us to know that it has been "here" all along—hollering and waving to get our undivided attention.

Spirit may be letting us know that our resistance is trying its patience.

How? Via the different energy pathways that relays spiritual information to us.

Chapter 36.

Avoiding Avoidance

The following skit is a composite of several actual case studies and does not represent a particular person.

Personality: I love my job. I get paid to do what I love.

Self: It's better if I avoid thinking about it.

Mind: I'd better not analyze it too much. Let me avoid it.

Body: My stomach hurts. I have acid reflux. I can't eat anything and my lower back hurts like hell.

Superego: Shh, don't cuss.

Ego: Get over it. I was just being expressive.

Observing Self: I am sick and tire of helping the same 'ole people and hearing their same old stories over and over again.

Personality: That is not true. I love my job.

Self: What exactly is my job?

Mind: If self doesn't know, I can't be bothered. Let me avoid it.

Psyche: My job descriptions instruct me to skirt around issues.

Observing Self: Skirting around issues *is* avoidance.

Ego: I am one of the most sought after speakers on Dependent Personality Disorders. I am booked six months in advance. I command top dollars at my speaking engagements.

Superego: Therefore I ought to know if I am avoiding issues or not.

Psyche: I take my job very seriously.

Self: What exactly is my job, again?

Heart: I want self to realize its job.

Mind: What's the fuss? It's simple. Just think it through.

Psyche: A master avoider conditioned me to deal with *every* obstacle I encounter in life by avoiding the heart of the matter.

Heart: Psyche knows squats about matters of the heart.

Ego: I wrote the definitive textbook on DPD. It is the standard textbook used in nearly every postgraduate PhD program.

Observing Self: Apparently, I am very skillful at taking what I know didactically and twisting it to suit my own distorted needs.

Mind: I facilitate psyche.

Psyche: Thanks for the assistance.

Personality: Don't forget. I put up a good front, too.

Self: What exactly is my job?

Mind: I hear an echo. Let me avoid it.

Ego: I aim to please.

Self: Ah, that may be my problem.

Superego: Aiming to please is a solid character reference. It is not a problem.

Heart: Trust me. I know. It's a problem.

Body: Trust heart. It is speaking the truth.

Self: I remember now. My job is not to please others.

Psyche: I better step in and do damage control. Let me avoid the topic.

Personality: I don't have to be a good little boy?

Observing Self: Psyche constantly operates as an eight-year old.

Superego: Good boys are rewarded by their fathers.

Observing Self: My father beat me every time he hit the bottle.

Self: I remember now.

Psyche: Self is starting to remember. I'm not doing my job very well. Let me avoid it.

Body: Let me tear his left rotator cuff so he'll need major surgery.

Ego: Brilliant. Distract him; then I can avoid it.

Psyche: Like I said, I take my job very seriously.

Self: My left shoulder hurts.

Observing Self: I need to make an appointment with the orthopedic surgeon.

Personality: Dr. Doolittle is a good friend of mine. He will fix me right up.

Self: What exactly is my job, again?

Mind: I hear an echo. Let me avoid it.

Spirit: Here we go again, around and around in a circle.

Personality: I love my job. I get paid to do what I love.

Spirit: This is becoming a hopeless case.

Soul: Don't give up.

Self: What exactly is my job, again?

Ego: I heal people.

Mind: I hear an echo. Let me avoid it.

Observing Self: That is not an echo. It is the continuous feedback loop of his avoidance tape.

Ego: I'm doing a great job.

Superego: I'm doing a great job.

Psyche: I've repeated those lines so often, I'd almost believe it if it weren't for the fact that I take my job very seriously.

Self: I feel so confused. I forgot again. What is my job?

Observing Self: Apparently I think it is my job to heal others. Yet I have barely begun the process of healing myself.

Superego: That's a rather harsh indictment.

Personality: People love me. I help them feel better about themselves.

Self: What about *my*self?

Ego: I am nothing without others.

Heart (gulp): That really hurt. Let me avoid it.

Spirit: The truth may hurt but it is better than living a lie.

Psyche: I will take that view under advisement.

Spirit: Don't take too long. The situation is getting desperate.

Mind: I agree. Let self take over as supervisor.

Ego (reluctantly): I will try to cooperate.

Heart: Or else, I will send him to the hospital with tachycardia.

Body: I don't want to die from a heart attack. Let's all work together.

Self: I am finally in charge, now.

Spirit: Finally, it's starting to make some sense in here.

Avoidance is the most widely used life strategy.

As a coping mechanism, avoidance only delays those existential issues which inevitably must be honestly faced in one's life.

Chapter 37.

Oblivious Oblivion

The following skit is a composite of several actual case studies and does not represent a particular person.

Heart: I feel so sad I can't get out of bed today.
Ego: I am oblivious.
Mind: I am oblivious.
Psyche: I prefer to be oblivious.
Observing Self: I am not oblivious.
Self: I'm glad someone in here is paying attention.
Superego: I must feed the baby.
Heart: Every time I look at her, I feel helpless.
Mind: I am oblivious.
Observing Self: I am not oblivious.
Self: My baby reminds me of myself as a baby.
Personality: That was a long time ago.
Mind: I can't remember.
Psyche: Babies are not conscious.
Instincts: Of course, babies are aware.
Common Sense: Just because I was preverbal, it doesn't mean I was oblivious.
Observing Self: I am not oblivious.
Heart: I was happy until mommy went away.
Personality: Which one?
Psyche: I am oblivious.
Observing Self: I am not oblivious.
Self: My biological mom.
Personality: I hardly knew her.

Psyche: I am oblivious.

Heart: I remember her.

Self: My adoptive mother turned out to be a total basket case.

Observing Self: Mom is neurotic.

Superego: Mom just wanted me to be very tidy and clean.

Personality: Mom puts herself together very nicely.

Psyche: I am fractured.

Observing Self: I have bipolar disorder.

Mind: No way. I am mentally very alert.

Ego: I am manic for a while and then I feel extremely depressed for a while.

Observing Self: I am not oblivious.

Superego: I do not have a mental illness.

Mind: A psychologist once told me I have one of the healthiest mental states he'd ever seen.

Self: He saw me during my high point.

Psyche: I was misdiagnosed.

Heart: If I am so mentally healthy, why do I feel so sad right now.

Instincts: Postpartum depression.

Observing Self: That's on top of undiagnosed bipolar disorder.

Psyche: I am oblivious.

Mind: I am oblivious.

Self: I wish I can afford to be oblivious.

Spirit: I need serious psychiatric intervention.

Soul: I won't be able to care for my baby like this.

Heart: I am so broken.

Observing Self: I am not oblivious.

Psyche: My husband is oblivious.

Ego: I will leave him in a month.

Superego: What will people think?

Personality: He is such a nice guy.

Observing Self: Just very oblivious.

Self: Is bipolar hereditary?
Mind: It can be.
Psyche: Will my baby have bipolar because of me?
Spirit: I have bipolar because of my biological mom.
Heart: Three generations of anguish.
Observing Self: I must get myself properly diagnosed and medicated.
Common Sense: That is the first sensible thought I've had in a long time.
Psyche: I am oblivious.
Mind: I am oblivious.
Ego: I am oblivious.
Personality: I am oblivious.
Self: Be oblivious but get help, anyway.
Spirit: I am here. I will stay.
Heart: I do not feel so alone.

Know the difference between the various roles that we must all play in life.

The essential self should not be confused with these roles.

Chapter 38.

Ignoring Ignorance

The following skit is a composite of several actual case studies and does not represent a particular person.

Observing Self: I'm using human psychology on a dog.

Personality: I don't like hurting Sparky's feelings.

Common Sense: Sparky is a dog, not a person.

Mind: I am ignorant.

Psyche: I don't like feeling ignorant.

Personality: I'll just ignore my feelings.

Superego: Sparky snarls, growls, nips and behaves badly around other dogs.

Ego: I don't get it. Sparky is so friendly around people and children.

Common Sense: He's not socialized.

Instincts: If a human was raised by a pack of dog who rarely let him interacted with people. When this human meets others of his kind, he will inappropriately resort to sniffing rumps and mounting behavior because that's the way he's been conditioned.

Mind: That sounds logical. I never thought of it that way.

Personality: A role reversal.

Observing Self: Correct. A dog raised by humans who hardly ever let the dog interact with others of his kind. This dog will be confused by normal doggie greetings. He will respond inappropriately to other dogs by yelping, recoiling, running away and/or withdrawing socially when he meets them.

Superego: So I should let Sparky sniff other dogs, even

though it triggers my social inhibitions.

Sparky: I wish she would stop treating me like a person.

Personality: I shower Sparky with tons of affection. I give him lots of treats. He sleeps in bed with me.

Observing Self: Sparky is fat. I give him too many cookies and overfeed him.

Ego: Sparky looks like a pin cushion.

Self: I am killing Sparky with love.

Common Sense: Obesity is not healthy.

Superego: He needs regular exercise.

Observing Self: Sparky must be walked a minimum of 30 minutes twice a day.

Ego: I don't have the time. I'll just ignore it.

Psyche: He gets to run around in a big backyard.

Common Sense: Walks are structured exercises. Besides he's not just randomly running wherever he wants and whenever he wants like he does in the yard.

Sparky: I'm a dog. I'm ruled by my nose. I need to get out; check out new scents; sniff things; and explore.

Self: The exercises will be good for me as well. It will help me slim down.

Ego: A win-win.

Mind: I've been ignorant and I'm starting to get it, now.

Common Sense: On the walks, discipline Sparky through the leash, like the way they do with horses.

Superego: Sparky must walk next to me or behind me and not ahead of me.

Personality: I passively hold the other end of the leash.

Observing Self: What if the leash was 25 feet long?

Sparky: She'd still just hold the other end of the leash.

Ego: Only an idiot would do that.

Common Sense: Apparently, I am an ignorant fool.

Instincts: When Sparky is ahead of me, it means he's the pack leader.

Personality: So what?

Sparky: I need my humans to be my pack leader. Otherwise, I'm confuse. Then, I can't help myself but act out.

Instincts: This is key. A domesticated dog living among humans must not take on the leadership position.

Common Sense: Especially when there are young children around.

Mind: Cesar Millan, the Dog Whisperer, says exercise, discipline and then affection brings psychological balance to a dog.

Common Sense: Cesar's methods make sense.

Personality: I like his TV show.

Superego: Cesar says being a calm and assertive pack leader really works wonders for dogs with behavior problems.

Mind: The same technique—being calm and assertive—works wonders on humans with behavior problems, also.

Ego: I don't want to change. I grew up with dogs all my life.

Observing Self: If I can't discipline myself, because I don't have a clue about my own psychology, then I can't be expected to train a dog.

Instincts: Out of ignorance, I mix up doggie psychology with human psychology.

Psyche: I have a headache.

Observing Self: The point of this lecture is so I would stop being an ignorant dog owner and, instead, be an educated pack leader for the sake of my beloved pooch.

Mind: That sounds logical.

Self: Maybe exercise and discipline, then affection, will rub off and I will be better at disciplining the kids.

Ego: They are a quite a handful.

Personality: That's because I don't set proper rules, limits and boundaries for them.

Heart: I feel sad and hopeless about it.

Psyche: Just ignore it.

Observing Self: Sparky's joints are stiff. His coat is dry. He has skin allergies. He eats poop and likes to roll in it, too.

Personality: I pretend I'm ignorant by ignoring what I know to be true about Sparky and my kids.

Psyche: Otherwise, I'd feel too guilty.

Sparky: My guts are a mess. She's been feeding me a corn-rich diet. I have a bad case of acidosis and halitosis.

Ego: Hey, a smart dog with a big vocabulary.

Common Sense: Give Sparky raw or cooked meat (chicken, turkey, lamb or beef) at least once a week.

Superego: I've been a vegetarian for twelve years.

Self: I meant, feed the meat to the dog, not myself.

Common Sense: It will be good for his health.

Ignorance is one of the most powerful blockers of life's energy pathways (see Chapters 18-23).

Many of us ignore our emotions.

We ignore our gut instinct.

We ignore the body's numerous signals of "dis-" eases.

We ignore our children.

We ignore our spouses and significant others.

We ignore our life's true purpose.

We ignore Spirit.

Spirit has this message for us: "do not come knocking on life's door, if all you are willing to do is ignore my subtle callings."

Granted in many parts of the world, people may be steeped in ignorance because of poverty and a lack of opportunities. Its afflictions, however, affect all of us because, in our ignorance, we do not bother to inform ourselves of the rules of the game.

In life, it is constructive to admit ignorance. *By our admission*, we can proceed to educate ourselves. If instead, we deny ignorance; we will have repeated an old pattern, again.

Repeating the same patterns in life will yield the same results—in life.

Act 8 .

News Flash

*Money, money, money
makes our world go around.*

Chapter 39.

Automating Life

A triumph of modern culture is the Industrial Revolution. This revolution in industry made mass production possible.

Mass productivity has left an indelible mark on modern culture because the lives of every single person on the globe is affected by it. Our lives are automated in quantities and speeds beyond our forefather's imagination.

Since the heydays of the Industrial Revolution, we have perfected our machines to automatically handle virtually every repetitive task. Many of our best machines have replaced human labor.

We expect our machines not to make mistakes.

We expect them not to deter from the tasks they were designed to perform.

Machines are not required to think, feel, emote or be aware. Their automation is what sets them apart from the other things in our world. Their automation serves us well.

Regardless of how much they may have improved the quality of modern life, automation and mass productivity are of no practical value in spiritual explorations.

Human beings are not machines.

Metaphoric inferences that suggest human productivity can be equated with mechanical outputs twist our minds. Take, for example, multi-tasking. The central processing units (CPUs) of computers are well equipped to handle millions of microprocessing operations per second—which we would want from our personal computers. Many of you have already caught on to the truth that multi-tasking does not suit human beings.

Our attempts to emulate mechanized productivity, such as multi-tasking, turn us into neurotics and maniacs. As a society, we expect instant gratification. We have short attention spans. We pop pharmaceutical-grade pills by the handfuls as if they were colored candy. We suffer the delusion that if anything and everything can be mass-produced, bought and sold, then things are disposable; and life, therefore, must be disposable, too. In turn, we, the masses, lose an intimate contact with our humanity.

We *must not* let commercial automations turn us into mechanical beings.

Just because our machines are automated, we should not live our lives on automatic pilot. When we are rote, we think and behave like robots. And as much as mechanization suits our machines, rote motions do not suit human beings—particularly not in the area of spiritual exploration. Robotic beings cannot be expected to explore, let alone appreciate, the mysteries of Spirit.

How sad it would be if Spirit's miracle of life transpired in a life that served no real purpose in the world?

Even a machine serves a purpose.

Because Spirit animates us, our automations ought to serve us and not the other way around.

We are, after all, here in body, heart and spirit to realize our humanity.

If anything, in the mechanized traffic of modern commerce, we would want to reverse this trend. As we free our time and energy because we do not have to grow our own food, built our own homes or make our own tools and furniture, we must utilize our newfound existential freedom to intimately contact with our humanity rather than wastefully cast our purposeful, and therefore spiritual, productivity into the wind.

Chapter 40 .

Culture and Being

Humanity's capacity for learning and transmitting knowledge to successive generations are recorded by and reflected in the diversity of human cultures that have come and gone.

A spirit of change is one of the discerning marks of modern culture.

Modernity's prolific cultural interplay of innovations, progress and revolutions are unrivaled in history. Modern art, quantum mechanics, relativity, genetic cloning, socialism, communism, the overthrow of socialism and a new cosmology are some examples. In the late 20th century especially , we witnessed diverse cultural phenomena accumulated critical mass, gained momentum and, seemingly from out of nowhere, an exponential explosion of new cultural transmissions suddenly catapults into our lives. When just a few minutes, hours, days, months or years ago, for all intents and purposes, these icons of pop culture were just taking shape in their embryonic forms. Take YouTube, MySpace and Facebook, for example.

As culture changes, so should our spiritual tools and traditions.

Gregory Bateson, in his cult classic, *The Selfish Gene*, coined the term "meme". He defines meme as "an unit of cultural transmission" or imitation. It derives from the Greek root "mimeme", as in mimesis and mimetic. The spread of catch phrases: inside out, mind over body, all natural; ideas: genome, quantum physics, virtual reality; tunes: Jesus Take the Wheel, Amazing Grace, Lucy in the Sky; and fashions: bell bottoms, Spandex, grunge in our pop culture are some examples he gives. (Bateson gave the general categories; I supplied the specifics.)

Culture is the tumultuous playground in which spiritual theories are tested, recorded, discarded and/or immortalized.

By the same token, according to Bateson's meme theory, spiritual imitations would also be propagated and catapulted into pop culture by similar means. Oprah's web launching of Eckhart Tolle's 10-week worldwide interactive course on *A Good Earth, An Awakening of Life's Purpose*, given free of charge, is an excellent example of a spiritual meme.

Keeping this in mind, out of this fertile dynamic, a modern culture of our spiritual being is born.

Chapter 41.

A Culture of Personality

The same economic cogwheels that replicate our tools and machines also produce a steady staple of celebrity personalities.

Our idolization of personalities over essential self is a reflection of our cultural disconnect with Spirit.

We live in a time where celebrities and personalities consume our airwaves. Our pop culture regularly serves up a healthy sampling of Hollywood, TV, sports, celebrity chef, journalist, music, rock star, hip hop, clothing, handbag and shoe designers, runway model and Internet personalities. Media darlings, wannabes, brats, hopefuls and even criminals, consume our media 24/7. We are fed a nonstop diet of celebrity personalities.

These icons of popular culture entertain us.

In order to be entertaining, they must have big personalities. They must be charismatic, likeable, easy on the eye, charming, outrageous, fun and bubbly. Because who would want to be entertained by a homebody, grump, total bore or sourpuss?

It is good for business to have a product associated with a famous face. In many ways, the commercial value of a product hinges on its publicity by a famous persona.

Celebrity personalities wield power in our society. Their prominent presence in many of our lives have turned celebrity personalities into role models—whether or not this was the intent of their publicist.

Herein lies an existential problem because generations of kids, who have not developed the life experiences and skills—as well as many of their parents, look up to our pop culture personality idols. Sadly, within some families, more intimate conversations are had about the escapades of media sirens, such as Paris Hilton, Lindsay Lohan, Britney Spears, Anna Nicole Smith and Madonna (until she outgrew her bad girl image) than with each other.

Behind the public image, what do we really know about how life is working for these highly visible personas? How well do their over-reliance on uppers, downers, painkillers, sedatives, anti-anxiety meds, booze, sex and living life at warp speed really get them through life? Why do so many of them check in and out of rehab as if this was a normal routine in every average Joe's life?

Sleek PR ploys apply temporary tourniquets to a life force that is in need of immediate resuscitation. Outside their publicists, managers and agents how do media personalities really feel about airing their dirty laundry for the whole world to see? Their marriages, clandestine affairs, custody battles, births and deaths smeared for the entire world to witness and judge. What human being, media savvy, celebrity status or not, wants his/her breakdown to be on public display? Who would want to be made into an object of media tug-and-war? How would anyone feel? After all, they are only human.

Do they cry themselves to sleep? Do they feel empty inside? Do they fill their emptiness by spinning out of control? Do they fall apart? Are they living a substantive, vital and essential life? Is the essential self standing firmly on home place and directing the onrushing traffic of life? How sad it is for entertaining personas to have camouflaged the essential self to such an extent that Spirit becomes lost to its resident human host?

Recall from Chapter 15 that the personality serves as a public camouflage for the private self. Therefore, although there is nothing wrong with having a personality, when the personality becomes the prominent image through which a celebrity finds glamour and fame, s/he will inevitably experience a spiritual crisis of personal identity at some time in life.

How would our children know any different but for what we model for them?

Along with tabloid gossip, do we inform our children that every celebrity personality must have a private side; because we all do? Every celebrity must eat, sleep, use the toilet, dress down, be a couch potato, has emotional and mental meltdowns, and experience losses and tragedies.

Should we not make it exceedingly clear to our youngsters that media, public relations and advertisement ought not violate or expose a person's private life to the public domain for the sake of making an easy buck?

Do we share the real answers to these sorts of questions with our children so that they gain perspective and context in their own lives and thereby pass our wisdom to future generations?

Stories of lost souls are tragedies. There is nothing glamorous about being memorialized in eternity because of an unfortunate drug overdose or severe split of personality.

Given that the media caters to changing social needs and not the other way around and, as absurd as the notion may be, perhaps we create a buzz so that, collectively, we do not have to face the pains of humanity.

I implore us to put entertaining twists in the context of our spiritual life.

It is not my intention to introduce a twist here.

Culture records humanity's histories.

When entertainment's amusements distract us from our spiritual roots, then it no longer qualifies as play. Rather, it serves to perpetuate a social legacy of ignorance, suffering and disempowerment.

Do we really want to be a culture remembered for its celebrity personalities?

Although popular culture seduces us into believing that a

likeable personality can get us through life, we should not permit cultural fads to determine the kind of connections we, each individually, make with Spirit.

We cannot look to people who are constantly in the public limelight to be our spiritual compass in life.

Chapter 42 .

Designer Lifestyle

I fear, for some of us, our lifestyles choices are literally killing us.

I am not being melodramatic or introducing a mythic metaphor. This is very serious business.

Up at the crack of dawn and on the go nonstop until the following sunrise—day after day, for years on end, like an overcharged energizer bunny—is simply impossible for the human body to sustain.

The human body, irrespective of Spirit's animating force, literally, factually, truthfully and mythically, at the cellular and physiological level of functioning, cannot handle our modern lifestyle stresses.

The thyroid gland burns out; because we are on the go, 18 to 20 hours out of 24.

The immune system begins to malfunction; because we have no idea how to really care for ourselves, both physically and emotionally.

The digestive system churns out too much acid; because we are constantly anxious.

We look to amphetamines and caffeine to rush us ahead; because if we did not, we would probably conk out and not wake up until a week later.

Sleeping pills and melatonin help to knock us out; because as much as we need it, we cannot unwind.

We get by on four to five hours of sleep for years on end; because we delude ourselves into believing that our productivity is the only measure of true success in life.

We put our personality split on display for millions worldwide to see; because their voyeuristic adoration fills an existential void that no amount of idolizing can satiate.

And we expect our poor hearts to keep pace; because we cannot feel its lonely exhaustion.

Tell me what is so glamorous about logging enough frequent flyer miles in a year to fly to the moon and back, five times over.

Work from 9-7 at a day job; eat dinner around midnight; party until 3-4 am; and start the same regiment again the next day is tiring enough just reading about it, let alone live it.

Don't like the look of a hooked nose? No problem. Get it surgically altered as many times as you would like, as long as you can afford it.

Don't like your marriage? No problem. Pay off the previous one and shop around for a beautiful new bride. There is a surplus of eligible singles who would be delighted to step in and help redo a botched matrimony.

Mirror, mirror on the wall does not lie about our over-tanned bodies, over-bleached hair, over-padded chests, overly made up faces, and our demeanors are made to match by being outrageously over the top.

Living out of suitcases, briefcases, plush tour buses and/or luxury hotel suits, we appear outwardly happy; but inside, we crave some good old-fashioned, homemade chicken soup for the soul.

I am not berating many of our wonderful modern luxuries and conveniences. I enjoy them as much as the next person.

I am also not on a witch-hunt for the many wonderful designers who greatly care about improving our quality of life.

And of course, we adopt varying lifestyles to suit climatic, geographic, regional and communal needs. Therefore, do not misconstrue, pigeonhole me with myopic viewing lenses and conclude that I am attacking every stylish novelty of pop culture.

I am simply pointing out that style and image are carefully crafted to sell.

The same economic cogwheels that replicate our tools and machines automatically produce a steady supply of designer lifestyles.

Styling life and the passions of the heart is a billion-dollar industry.

Lifestyles are life's luxuries. Style glamorizes our most basic needs. We style food; shoes; handbags; cars; clothes; our bodies; our homes; sex; lingerie; travel; vacation; and just about everything that has to do with luxurious living. We equate style with good taste, impeccable manners, flawless grace, sophistication, pedigree breeding and high-society class.

Some of us are so caught up with "styling" our personalities that we forget self and Spirit are the most stylish life player of them all.

Style is to life as the personality is to the self. When a lifestyle becomes the person's identity, there is a loss of identity. With a loss of self-identify, Spirit is also lost in the process. When Spirit is lost to a soul, no amount of "styling" will make life glamorous or beautiful.

Let there be no doubt: the hottest, single most desirable and fabulous style of life, by far, is to be alive.

I am not introducing a twist here.

I implore us again to put entertaining twists in the context of our spiritual life.

Spirit governs over life and death. Such matters are paramount. They are so important, any stylistic trend pales by comparison.

Staying healthy is stylish. Staying alive is far more stylish.

Truth be told, one's health in all respects—physical, mental, psychological, emotional, as well spiritual—is the most accurate barometer of spiritual intimacy.

Overall health cannot twist the truth out of how well a lifestyle is really working for a person.

Lifestyle choices should be secondary to life itself. When lifestyle becomes more important than life itself, Spirit will not just give an occasional silent grunt. Spirit will be compelled to make us aware of its displeasures.

Interior design one's self from the inside out instead of dressing the outside with designer brands. Spirit wants us to be so spiritually enriched that we no longer required designer "things" to make us shine with high-society style.

Common sense and psychological, emotional and mental wellbeing are deliberately left out of this "stylicious" discussion, because these topics will take up another volume.

Stage 4.

Life 101

Act 9 .

Back to Basics

Looking for answers.

Chapter 43.

Enigma

The playing field beyond the ordinarily physical poses an enigma for humanity.

Those of us who move on beyond our physical forms, we take with us the ultimate, yet unsubstantiated, answers to the enigma, with no way to relay them back to the terrestrial dimension.

And even if an answer could miraculously make its way back to us, its message would appear so extraordinarily vacuous and surreal to 99.9% of us that most would probably it as a fanciful figment of our imagination

The nature of the enigma is like a self-perpetuating puzzle for which no conclusive resolutions can ever be reached. Yet, the nature of the enigma compels humanity to explore its mysteries.

Spirit's incredible breadth—and breath—is precisely what makes the enigma of life so mysterious.

Even though its answers escape our concrete fact gathering, journalistic documentation, tangible verification, scientific research and repeatable reproducibility, humanity continually searches to resolve the mystery.

In this quest to understand the enigma and regardless of the inevitability of the plight, no one is spared.

Ask heart for the real answers.

Chapter 44.

Spiritual Diversity

According to the world census gathered by The World Factbook of the Central Intelligence Agency (updated on June 19, 2007), Christians comprise 33.03% of the world—of which Roman Catholics make up 17.33 %, Protestants 5.8%, Orthodox 3.42% and Anglicans 1.23%. Muslims make up 20.12%, Hindus 13.34%, Buddhists 5.89%, Sikhs 0.39%, Jews 0.23%, other religions 12.61%, nonreligious 12.03% and atheists 2.36% (a 2004 estimate).

How does humanity go about arriving at a common ground, given our differing belief systems?

How do our spiritual views differ?

How do we go about articulating the similarities and differences of our varying views?

Would we understand one another to the extent that we amicably agree to differ?

Ought we not at least be able to converse and understand one another using a common standard—albeit they may be spoken in diverse languages?

Let us give praise to diversity: Baha'i, Buddhist, Christian, Confucian, Druidic, Hindu, Islamic, Jainist, Jewish, Mandaean, Native American Indian, Mayan, Pre-Egyptian, ancient Egyptian, Sumerian, Rastafarian, Shinto, Sikh, Taoist, Zen, theosophical, shamanistic, naturalist, tribal, indigenous, aboriginal, voodoo, ancient, modern and apocalyptic views list a partial chronicle of humanity's differing spiritual relationships to the enigma.

In our searching for answers to the enigma, we must not offend or malign some ones else's choice of and to faith.

Throughout human history, those who felt that it was their moral duty to defend their passionate spiritual and religious views from dissenting parties have waged countless wars. Today, in many parts of the world, this is still an ongoing process.

Spiritual and religious factions have generated pain, conflict and needless suffering. Enough is enough.

Before attempting to unravel the enigma, if all factions would agree to one constant: That we are all searching to understand and realize our highest purposes in life.

That in such a discourse and discussion, what is purposeful in life for one person may not and should not be right for an other.

When it comes to Spirit, an answer to the mystery lies in our capacity to tolerate and embrace the diversity of our cultural and religious perspectives.

Ask heart for the real answers.

Chapter 45.

Words or Deeds

Language is our main vehicle for expressing to one another what we mean.

Through language, spiritual traditions are passed onto each successive generation.

In this area our language seems to have a built-in propensity for introducing more paradoxes than offer concrete answers.

I wonder:

What would "angel" be to a Buddhist, Muslim, agnostic or atheist?

What would "guru" or "karma" be to a Mormon?

What would "compassion" be to a Orthodox Jew?

What would "metaphysical" be to a Shinto priest or Hindu yogi?

What would a "ghost" or "apparition" be to the different peoples of the contemporary world?

What would "spirit" be to a Native American Indian?

What would "soul" be to a Catholic or Tibetan Buddhist?

Do their uses in oriental traditions, for example, Buddhism and Hinduism, differ from occidental traditions, such as Catholicism and Christianity?

Why are there two different words in English for "them" spirit and soul "things", if each word does not appear to signify separate and distinctively unique functions in the world?

If there are distinctions, specifically what are they?

How is it that we name the "Holy Spirit", or "Holy Ghost" as it was commonly referred to prior to the 20th century, but we do not speak of a "Holy Soul"?

What is "lord" to a Zulu?

What is "god" to an agnostic or atheist?

What would "Allah" be to an Evangelist?

Could it be conceivable that asking someone to "pray" may be taken as an offense?

When Christians pray to the Lord for absolution of terrorism and Muslims pray to Allah for absolution of capitalism, whose prayer will be granted and by which divine source?

Could it be possible that pop culture's cult fascination with aliens and outer space visitors mythically represent a modern-day metaphor for Spirit?

When Scottie "beams 'em up" at the request of Captain Kirk, are sentient beings spatially transported "Across the Universe", with or without the help of advanced ET technologies?

Are Star Trek and Star Wars groupies manifesting an "alien" sort of quest, which U2-384 would wholeheartedly appreciate?

Those people who do not customarily lace their speech with spiritually loaded catchwords should we automatically assume that they are not spiritually inclined, whereas those whose speech is liberally peppered with them are vastly more spiritual?

Our words, instead of facilitating common understanding, may make for more confusion, disagreements and differences to what is already enigmatic.

Chapter 46.

Game Theories

In spirituality, suppositions are referred to as beliefs.

Science refers to its hypothetical suppositions as theories.

One of our preeminent theoretical physicists, Stephen Hawkin in his bestselling book, *A History of Time*, tells us that science does not offer proofs, only theories.

Systematic methodologies form unified standards and precedents in science. We value the systematic guidelines of science, because the intent of science is to solve mysteries for the benefit of humanity.

Science has its share of theories.

Why not spirituality?

Who is to say that science has a monopoly on systematic explorations?

Why do we have differing standards for the systematic study of *scientific* beliefs and metaphysical explorations of *spiritual* theories?

Presently, science and spirituality do not mix company. The study of science is not integrated into spirituality and spirituality is not integrated into the study of science.

By adopting a *systematic* study for spirituality, we would progress our understanding of spiritual mysteries, because the intent of any systematic inquiry is to solve mysteries for the benefit of humanity.

Before we can hope to soar to the heavens, we must begin the process of spiritual discovery by firmly planting our feet on solid ground.

For starters, any systematic exploration must begin with a set of vocabulary, word definitions, terms and concepts.

Because how else would we know we are speaking about the same thing, let along reach a common understanding and/or consensus?

In our looking for answers to the enigma, methods for studying science and spirituality can share common pedagogic roots. All it takes is a shift in our perspective.

Chapter 47.

Factions

How many crusades, inquisitions, ethnic cleansings and genocides must occur before we learn to settle our spiritual differences?

Truth be told, human beings kill other human beings over their spiritual beliefs.

Throughout recorded history, different factions have fought over their sovereign rights to practice the spiritual tradition of their choice, while, at the same time, persecuting others for those same rights.

Factions fight over which version of the game is right?

Which version is better and more powerful?

Whose god is the "real" god?

This may be an uncomfortable topic that some seekers of spirituality would prefer to ignore, avoid or deny. Historical data do not lie. Therefore, we would do well to take these factual data to heart, especially in an introductory exploration into our spiritual nature.

Our existential ignorance, spiritual oblivion and mental resistance cannot be expected to unravel the profundity of the enigma.

Science cannot prove the existence of Spirit—neither can religion or spirituality. A need for concrete proof will only retard our spiritual progress.

Spiritual exploration values life more than winning an argument over who is right.

Any attempts to popularize universal laws for the sake of spirituality should, at the very least, not create factions in the world.

Our dissent, confusion and misgivings may be furthering the mystery.

The cost of which is a cultural loss of our spiritual sense of life's purpose.

Chapter 48 .

A United Human Race

Spirit is an enigma. The finality of this statement, humanity can agree on.

Spiritual explorations ought to be a liberating and creative endeavor.

Our common bond of humanity links that which we share than that which divides us.

We are not perfect.

We are all in the same boat.

A compulsion to realize answers to the enigma is spiritually built into every fiber of our essential nature.

In honor of the gift of life, let us not denigrate, degrade or destroy each other over our views on the right to life.

In our looking for answers to the enigma, humanity ought not fight or kill each other for the sake of our different views regarding the forces that grant us life.

After all, given that each life is so very precious, why fight or disagree over who's got it "right" or "wrong", when we cannot even begin to figure out how to respect and value life without letting our bruised egos get in the way?

In Spirit's view, our killing one another over whose version of life is the right version is like fighting over whether heads or tails is the correct representation of a coin. The truth is both are.

Could arriving at a peaceful settlement be part of humanity's spiritual quest?

Until that time, when it comes to exploring spiritual mysteries, the motto: "agree to disagree" is most fitting.

In looking for answers to the enigma, we may never arrive at a consensus.

Perhaps part of the charm of the enigma is that we will not ever conclusively solve or realize these sorts of mysteries.

These are not philosophical propositions.

My desire for this series of four volumes is to demystify the mystery; to bridge discord and friction; and to open exploration, reflection and discovery to every single human being who seeks to master the game of life.

Chapter 49.

Game Master

There can be only one answer to the question: who made up the game of life?

The master of the game of life is god.

A built-in rule of the game is that, in our capacity as mortals, we cannot hope to proof beyond a shadow of a doubt the existence of god. Our science cannot prove the existence of god—neither can our religion nor spirituality.

A need for concrete proof will only retard our spiritual progress.

Therefore, what we say about god must be taken at faith.

Battles waged by human egos about divine forces have no place in any spiritual exploration. Exploration implies a spirit of openness, acceptance and tolerance.

God stands for the creator of everything that exists in the universe—including the enigma behind many of god's rules and laws.

God lives outside the scope of life, as we know it.

God in its infinite wisdom knew what it intended when it created the world.

God knew what it intended when it created humanity.

God knew what it intended when it created religion and spirituality.

God created Spirit just as god created humanity.

God is the guiding force behind Spirit's mysterious ways.

By god's creation of humanity, Spirit is vested in every sphere of our body, mind, psyche, heart and soul.

Our making an intimate contact with Spirit spontaneously ensures that we make an intimate contact with the divine force which created Spirit and humanity.

Why? Because, by virtue of its animating energy, Spirit is closer to god than we are.

God is like a master of ceremony presiding over the game. Ceremony refers to divine rules, laws and rituals. Think of them as the unwritten and unspoken "invisible" directions for the game.

The game master does not partake in the playing of the game, just as Bob Barker (The Price Is Right) and Alec Trebek (Jeopardy) do not partake in playing the games that they MC. (Game show names which, by the way, are comical spoofs on versions of the game of life that can be played.)

These examples must not be taken literally. We do not typically think of god as the creator of games. Typically, we think of games as the sort of communal activities that are lighthearted, fun and serving the purpose of entertainment, amusement and play.

Some would have us believe that god, being the supreme creator of all things that exist, has a vested interest in more serious, profound and sacred matters.

We can assume that God has a pretty good sense of humor, is generally very tolerant of our simple ways and unconditionally accepts us the way it created us. Nearly everyone who is blessed by divine grace will attest to these characterizations of god.

Viewing religious and spiritual traditions as game theories and god as the game master may be unconventional. It may cause some controversy in some traditional circles.

However, to view god as a game master and MC makes the prospect of having an intimate contact with god a little less unattainable, formidable and impossible to sustain.

Such a mind-set neutralizes traditional associations. This may have the ripple effect of opening up the process, which might make the quest more accessible to every human being.

Depending on our varying philosophical, cultural and religious orientations, god present different views to the different peoples of our world.

Our differing answers pave a foundation for our spiritual explorations.

Those who cannot hold to a spirit of tolerance have more stakes in being right (ego) than expressing a profound love for humanity (god).

The supreme being who magnanimously created the universe and all of reality as we presently know it to exist would have the generosity of spirit to patiently wait and enable us to arrive at spiritual truths without our heated discussions and debates about it.

One of the goals of this book is to show that spiritual explorations can break ground without our debates about god.

Why? Because, too many human lives have been needlessly taken in the names humanity gives its gods.

Truth be told, human beings kill other human beings over their beliefs in god. Some of the bloodiest wars and battles have been waged over mankind's right to worship god—or more accurate, which god.

As such, the word god appears in lower case because this introductory exploration does not advocate one particular supreme being. Our overuse has turned the capitalized version of our name for god into something that is nearly meaningless.

God is not an abstraction. God is a name we give to the one who is sacred.

God is genderless. When it comes to the supreme creator, the issue of male or female is a moot point. If something as simple as a coin can be viewed from several multiple angles, then by comparison, god must total an infinite number of complex angles, of which gender is about as irrelevant as how god created all that we know to exist from nothing.

If Spirit is the animating energy of life and god is the creator of life, then our quandary over the enigma was, is and will be god's intention.

The bulk of the enigma involves humanity's interpretations, understanding and acceptance of god's rules, laws and rituals for the game.

To partake in the game of life without having an intimate relationship with the game master creates a spiritual crisis within the soul. Because without *a priori* knowledge of the game master's setup, how can anyone get a handle on playing the game, let along hope to win?

Chapter 50 .

Instruction Manual

Without our direct access to a universal instruction manual, or at least without our ability to agree on the definitive manual given to us by god, our misunderstandings, misinterpretations, mistranslations and/or misuses may have inadvertently, and unnecessarily, caused more mysteries to be created.

What if life came with an instruction manual? After all, every "thing" of practical use in our lives does.

What would be in the manual?

How detailed of a manual must it be?

Would it be easily understandable?

Who should its target audience be?

Everyone; a select few; children five years and older; infants and newborns?

What universal language should it be written in?

Who would write it?

Would it need to be translated?

Does it need to be deciphered, i.e. decoded, before it can be translated?

If it needs to be deciphered and decoded, who can we entrust with the job?

If it needs to be translated, who can be entrusted with the job?

Would the translator and decoder need special education?

What sort of education?

Would the education include a person's life experiences and life skills?

Must it include scholarly, academic, intellectual, theological and/or spiritual expertise?

Why would a scholar or theologian's view carry more existential weight or be more valid than each of our individual views regarding this matter?

Would the manual help us understand the purpose of life?

Would it come with a list of basic vocabulary, as any well-written and systematic manual should?

If we had a glossary of terms, would it help us solve the mysteries concerning Spirit, the animating energy force of life?

How many of us are in need of such a manual?

How would it change our lives?

Most of us would want life's crucial answers succinctly written down and handed to us on a silver platter. For it to tell us what is the purpose of life; how to play the game of life; how to excel at life; how to excel at playing the game of life; and instruct us on how to genuinely contact Spirit, soul and god.

If we had the manual in hand, would we be searching as hard as some of us are or feel as lost?

How well would we follow its instructions?

Would most of us follow every instruction to the letter or would we only use it as a preliminary guide?

Would the instructions be in the form of explicit rules, laws, doctrines or commandments, or would it be written in mysterious codes?

Would Spirit continue to mystify us in the same way that it does now?

Think about it. Which versions of "instructions" you follow dictate what you will get out of life.

When it comes to an instruction manual on life, there are so many unanswered and unanswerable questions?

What are the answers?

Whence would the most accurate and truthful answers come?

Would Spirit write in its own voice?

Would Spirit define every minute detail?

Would Spirit break down every complexity into discrete units?

Is the Holy Bible the definitive manual?

What about the Koran, Torah, Tipataka or Vedas?

Would this definitive manual give us explicit instructions on how to get to that everlasting place after death?

And cash in on the promise of an everlasting life?

Would it clearly spell out our actions and consequences?

Would it tell and show us, as well as enforce the punitive actions and consequences when we violate its instructions?

Would the manual hold up through the test of time?

For example, would it be as pertinent 6,000 years ago, today or 65,000 years from now?

Would the manual incite pedagogic wars, crusades and battles?

If so, what does that say about the manual's point of origin?

Does the manual instruct us to value life over dogma and self-righteousness?

Or, vice versa?

Varying groups throughout recorded history have made claims to their "ownership" of the definitive instruction manual on life.

How is it that something that should be an inherent part of our very essence and nature become shrouded in so much mystique, to the extent that its mysteries are relegated to the escutcheon of secret societies, privileged initiates, guru masters and divining saints, instead of being available to all?

How much would such a manual cost?

How should it be marketed?

Given what it is—an instruction manual on life—should it be provided free-of-charge to every single person, regardless of their status in life, educational or occupational backgrounds?

What department of our global society would be responsible for overseeing its collective distribution to the masses?

How would its distribution be monitored?

By the government, the clergy, educators, bookstores or some specialized branch of society that has yet to be created?

What would be the political, philosophical, cultural, religious and/or spiritual implications?

What sort of an instruction manual would stop us from killing one another over our beliefs?

Who is to judge whose representation is the right one?

Clearly mankind cannot make such a judgment.

Life would be less enigmatic if only humanity would agree on the version of the instruction manual that actually came directly from god.

In looking for answers to the enigma, our answers can only be as good as our questions.

Ask heart for the real answers.

Chapter 51 .

Traditions

Humanity's quest to unravel the enigma leaves us with a richness of spiritual traditions.

The spiritual view advanced in this series of books makes the following distinctions:

Spirit is the energy.

Soul is the source of the energy.

Energy stands for the life-giving *spirit* of the essence. The source refers to essence itself.

God is the creator of the energy and source.

When it comes to spiritual exploration, let us keep it simple and basic.

For starters, every spiritual tradition that has survived the test of endurance over time must universally address a few very simple and basic topics. For example:

What happens to us after we die?

Where do we "go"?

Is there another plane beyond the earthly one?

What is the nature of this other plane beyond the earthly one?

What is the relationship between our deeds in life and their consequences in the afterlife?

What are the rules of rewards and punishments?

Who makes up the rules?

Who oversees the rules?

Where do we look for the real answers?

Who has the real answers—mortals or immortals?

What do we call this "thing" that lives on after our bodies physically expire?

Is there such a "thing" or is life simply a matter of "what we see is what we get and the end is our final end"?

In our earliest traditions, survival issues such as keeping warm and having enough to eat took on paramount importance. In subsequent traditions, the sun, or Sol, was worshipped, as both god and the life-animating force. Perhaps, this is how the word "soul" came about. That the sun sustains life, as we know it to exist on this planet, is undeniable.

In subsequent traditions, mankind's more savage and bestial nature may have require it to be balanced by laws, justice, morality, ethics, etiquettes, manners, and other refined attributes of civilized cultures and societies.

Each human civilization heralds a distinctive philosophical view. Philosophy is intricately linked to the development of religion.

Until very recently, religion and spirituality typically evolved together. Thus, we have acquired a tradition in which spirituality and spiritual expressions share common linguistic roots, philosophical origins and popular uses with religion.

Every tradition must rely on language, be it written or oral, for the cultural transmission of its unique stance.

Tens of thousands of books have been written about the historical, theological, liturgical, philosophical, anthropological, sociopolitical and cultural traditions presented by the Bible, Koran, Talmud, Torah, Tipataka, Vedas, Tao Te Ching, I Ching, Confucian Analects and other major religious and spiritual texts. Thousands more books will be written in the future.

Because this book is not intended as a scholarly treaties, except for a few examples below, the factually pertinent specifics on spiritual and religious traditions I leave to the more qualified academicians and scholars, given that their expertise in these areas are, by far, more studied than mine.

Various traditions have pitched their versions of spiritual truths. They share commonalities.

From the Christian tradition, we have Genesis Chapter 2, verse 7, "And the Lord God formed man of the dust of the ground, and breathed into his nostrils the breath of life; and man became a living soul." In other words, God formed the body of mankind from earthly material. God breathed the breath of life (or Spirit, as it is defined in this book) into the nose (a portal of respiration) of the body of mankind. Whereupon mankind became alive. Are these words to be taken literally as factually accurate historical data or as mythic metaphors? Does it universally represent the spiritual beliefs of all of mankind?

According to Deepak Chopra, in Indian tradition, he tells us in *How to Know God,* the soul has two parts: Jiva and Atman. He writes that Jiva "refers to the individual soul ... and makes a long journey through many lifetimes until it reaches full realization of God." Jiva would correspond to Spirit in this text. Atman does not partake in any journey because it is made of the same pure spirit essence as God. "Atman cannot change in any way. It never reaches God because it never left in the first place ... There is no good approximation for Atman in the West, and many people might wonder why the soul has to be divided in this way."

Shen is a keyword in Chinese philosophy, religion and holistic healing practices. Its multiple meanings developed over three millennia. Eleven associated meanings can be loosely given for it, from "spirit, god, demeanor, supernatural, esteem, govern, cautious, exhibit, clever, portrait to surname."

The passing of our knowledge relies on language for its transition through successive generations. Just as a person's biographical history is uniquely individualized, cultural history also provides specific contexts. These contextual variations color language.

Traditionally, the West tends towards analysis. Traditionally, an analytic approach cannot hope to uncover spiritual truths.

In the West, a system for science and a platform for spirituality polarized these two methods for uncovering universal laws.

Traditionally, the East tends towards synthesis. Traditionally, a synergistic approach sees no division between the body, mind, heart, spirit and divine grace. In many non-western traditions, such as Native American Indian, Tibetan Buddhist, Polynesian aborigines and tribal African, the boundaries between physical and metaphysical blur. A spirit of unifying inclusion, rather than compartmentalization and segregation, is sought and honored.

Cultures worldwide influence one another. This is especially true in view of technology's globalization of our planet.

Those of us who seek to bridge the gap between analysis and synthesis must embark on our own personal pilgrimages to recover a sense of spiritual wholeness in our hearts and souls.

Spiritual explorations must develop from a solid foundation of tradition.

East or West, traditions are recorded history.

Traditions are invaluable.

Traditions provide guidance.

Traditions leave us with historical lineage and context.

Tradition provides us with a historical platform that informs and influences our current thinking.

Traditions cannot and should not be ignored or dismissed.

Traditions must be honored and respected.

The distinction I make between spirit and soul may seem inconsequential and pedantic. However, in the context of our modern understanding of energy, it *is* necessary. (I make a case for this in my book, *Riding Quantum Waves*.) Imagine the systematical study of the behaviors and characters of energy particles and waves without distinctions made regarding gravity, electromagnetism, strong and weak forces—the four forces of the universe as we presently presume there to be only four.

Traditions, however, do not become long-standing emblems of culture if they are not flexible and resilient to change.

Change cannot take place without what has come before.

I am writing about revolutions in a mystical tradition.

To revolve is to rotate in a circular pattern.

Although we typically associate social revolutions with an overhaul of existing and pre-existing ideologies, over great periods of time, occurring patterns will repetitively emerge.

Like a perpetually turning wheel, with each complete rotation, progress is made.

Revolutions, therefore, implies a respect for what has come before.

When traditions become fixated, unyielding, fanatical, authoritarian and rigid, they turn into dogmas. Like a favorite old pair of running sneakers for which the treads eventually lose traction, the arch support gives way and the body disintegrates beyond repair, traditions can cause us to become stuck in a rut.

To stop revolving is to be stuck on one point of the circle—of life.

If we were to come back, say three million years from now, we may find that cracking the basic codes to the enigma still elude mortal inquiries. Hopefully, however, we will have advanced our views.

Are religious and spiritual explorations implicitly one and the same? No.

One need not be religious to explore Spirit. Being alive is, in and of itself, requirement enough.

We are each born with our spiritual roots intact.

First: find and remember your spiritual roots and all of the traditions that go along with it.

Then, pick and choose from any spiritual traditions that enhance who you are.

Keeping an open mind may be the only prerequisite for revolutions in Spirit.

After all, Spirit must have revolved around the circle of life a few revolutions since the birth of the cosmos.

Act 10.

In Truth

Let the chips fall where they may.

Chapter 52 .

No Directions

Something like this has probably happened to every one of us. We are in a new city. We may have just moved or are on vacation there. We can't quite orient ourselves. We turn and ask the first stranger we meet for directions. We assume that they must have a clearer sense, because they live there.

We merrily trot off, only to find out twenty blocks later that this person, who seemed quite friendly, articulate and mentally lucid, jovially gave us the wrong directions. Instead of south, they steered us east.

Life is like this.

Life does not come with a set of clearly written, step-by-step directions.

When we feel disoriented, we are prompted to turn to other people for directions. We look for reassurances from all the wrong places and from people who have not a clue that life must be lived with meaning, purpose and passion. We assume they would know better than us because either they seemed to have lived a productive long life, hold socially important positions, give the impression they are divinely directed, and/or they just sound reasonable.

More often than not, when it comes to solving spiritual mysteries, another human being is simply another one of us. Their sense of direction in life may be just as disoriented and confused as ours—regardless of their apparent statures in life.

Life is like a big jigsaw puzzle. Except, the pieces are not tidy little cutouts that fit neatly together. The box cover gives no picture guides so that, at least, we can follow along.

No explicit directions on "how to" are given.

The process is not interactive or mutually reciprocal—meaning that the jigsaw puzzle of life does not have a built-in mechanism to let us know if we are headed in the right direction. The label on the box reads: "Figure it out yourself!"

Perhaps, should directions for life be granted, direction number one would clearly spell out that: as much as we might wish for it, the only directions in life we can really count on is the one directed by our intimate contact with Spirit.

If Spirit could instruct us, it would probably give us one very simple life-enhancing direction:

"Every day, consciously make an effort
"to stop"—in your life—
for a minimum of 10 minutes.
Go somewhere quiet where you can be alone.
There should be no outside disturbances.
Stop your bad habit of running after time.
Forget about the double-booked appointments
you tightly squeezed in and must rush to in half an hour.
Put your precious pet projects on temporary brain-hold.
You do not need to chant, hum, recite incantations,
pray, or perform any kinds of ceremonial rituals.
You can exhale. You need to exhale. Exhale!
See how the next breath, of life,
spontaneously flows into your lungs.
The whole point is to give yourself permission
to take a break from the busyness—
or is it business?—of your life."

Chapter 53.

No Guarantees

The only guarantee we can expect in life is death.
This harsh and unyielding condition of life must be explicitly named in any spiritual exploration because it is blatantly self-evident, ubiquitous and nonreversible.

Life is a game of chance. Accidents happen. The most worthy and valiant of us have been known to die under horrific circumstances. A terminally ill child dies before her parents. A speeding drunk driver strikes a family of four dead. A municipal bridge collapses during rush hour killing seventy-five unsuspecting commuters. A stray bullet from rivaling gangs kills an innocent 18-month old child. Two jumbo jets are flown into the World Trade Center and heroes who sacrificed their lives divert the third one meant for the Pentagon.

In most instances, we literally get only one chance and that is all there is to it.

When shit happens, we perceive this "no-guarantee" clause of life's contract to be cruel and unjust.

Deep down in our heart and spirit, all of us must inevitably concede to the game of survival. Few of us need convincing, although most of us prefer not to dwell on it obsessively.

A simple message of: "life comes with no guarantees" is enough.

Just tell it—or would it more likely be, sell it—the way it is.

For some of us, by giving us the gift of life, we ungraciously expect an exchange of equal value to be made. Where, by our simply being here, we are automatically guaranteed to live a life full of purpose—without our having to work at it.

This unrealistic guarantee implies that just because the fragmented parts of our psyches, minds and personalities delude ourselves into believing that we are spiritually special, Spirit will therefore keep us alive at all cost. We are unwilling to confront or challenge the existential cost of our spiritual delusions.

Although our fear of death may trigger an array of primal reflexes, threats of hell and damnation are not the best spiritual motivators.

The spiritual language chosen should make simple common sense to everyone and not be so removed from ordinary reality that it takes an esteemed alien anthropologist like U2-358 to decode its celestial messages.

Spiritual guarantees, when provided, should not talk down to us. Because when that unforeseeable moment unexpectedly slams into us, no amount of bargaining, compromising, regretting, redeeming, lamenting or life insurance policy of any price will change survival's inevitable outcome. That is a spiritual guarantee you can take to the bank!

A sufficiently developed spiritual outlook will provide us with a small cushion of comfort in the face of life's built-in Faustian clauses.

Whether we want to or not, we, by the simple fact of occupying a body and our being alive, we are registered participants in the game of life and death.

The one guarantee may be: do not play around with life and death. That domain falls under the strictest of laws and is enforced by the true enforcer of spiritual laws. Should 'it' deem it necessary to unleash its wrath, let no mortal fool stand in its way.

Chapter 54.

Biographical History

Nature abhors a vacuum.
Nothing in life can happen in pure isolation.
Everything that happens in life is relational.

Engaging in Spirit's mysteries cannot take place abstractly. The reason being: without a biographical history, there would have been no life.

Without biographical context, as far as Spirit is concerned, any spiritual exploration—introductory or otherwise—will have been done in vain.

Our biographical histories are as unique and individual as our fingerprints.

There are our genetic predispositions.

There are our ethnic, national and cultural heritages.

There are our upbringing and education.

There are our life experiences and how they shaped us.

They are the particular set of circumstances that determines how we got to be where we are in life and where we are headed.

Our biographical histories provide the context for each of our lives. Each history is the culmination of life experiences acquired in a lifetime.

Along with our personal histories come personal experiences. These experiences are so unique and individualistic; they cannot be duplicated, replicated or authentically understand by anyone else but the person who has lived that particular life in that particular body.

Let a distinction be clearly made here: the details of biographical history do not define who we are.

For example, many biographies and memoirs have been written about presidents, politicians, entrepreneurs, celebrities, visionaries and those whose life stories peek the public's interest. Spirit, however, does not stand on ceremony.

Where Spirit is concerned, the notoriety of a person's professional achievements and our taking an interest in their biographies are not prerequisites for enrollment in the worldwide classroom of spiritual exploration.

Biographical history may shape and mold a person. It may greatly influence a person. A person's essential nature, meaning self, spirit and soul, however, is *not* defined by his/her biographical history—in other words, "what you do", for a living, and who you have been, in your life.

History flows forth from having lived and not the other way around.

Each person accumulates millions of little pieces of the giant jigsaw puzzle. Those of us who are privy to the pieces of our own puzzle have a clearer sense of the big picture and, because of this, we can know our true purpose in life. For some of us, our existential intactness may have shattered. The many pieces may be scattered, buried and hidden in the deepest reaches of our souls; so much so, our existential gaze fixates on single blades of grass.

Context provides the concrete references out of which life makes sense and takes on meaning. Journalists, detectives, clergy and mystery solvers are well acquainted with the reality that behind every human story, contextual circumstances have the power to influence life's outcomes. Because in life, context is, quite literally, all that really matters.

Repeat: context matters

When we begin to gather, arrange and make sense of the jigsaw pieces of our lives, our view of single blades of grass turns into majestic trees of life which, through commitment and dedication over time, inevitably evolve into cosmic knowledge. In this process, we are essentially making an intimate contact with Spirit.

Needless to say, our spiritual growth, development and maturity are an essential part of our biographical history.

Chapter 55.

Complexities

Life is complex.
 Our lives are complex.
Modern life is complex.

There are our jobs, promotions, demotions, relocations, financial security, national, state, city, local and international politics, elections, zoning issues, school boards, schooling, our kids, health, fitness, daily exercise, diet, recreation, vacations, economic incentives, green house effects, investments, savings, debts, mortgages, bank loans, alimony, patrimony, romances, prenuptials, marriage vows and on-and-on the list goes.

In our social interactions, there are many unspoken codes of conduct. The codes are like the rules of a game. The codes and rules are complex. By and large, many of our life skills concern how well we have learned to navigate, manipulate and play the social game. Although many are silent codes, on occasion, speaking about them may even be construed as a taboo—which is in itself coded.

It would be an understatement to say that we are complex creatures.

At the heart of our complexities are the extraordinarily diverse range of human experiences and responses that uniquely characterize the humanness of our nature.

A paradox inherent in spiritual exploration lies in our complexity.

We live in a culture built on proof.

We want things in life certified. We want things verified. We want to be able to reproduce, replicate and record life. We want life's events documented. It would appear that we seek factual certainty in and out of life. This mind-set complicates modern life. Because of it, we also continually seek more time-efficient and convenient ways to simplify our busy and convoluted lives.

Our drive to make simple and tangible those mystifying intangibles of life complicates everything.

In comparison to the complexities of our lives, Spirit is exponentially much more complex.

The mechanism whereby Spirit sustains life in a physical body must be so complex; science has probably uncovered just a smidgeon of a speck of its limitless operations. How Spirit goes about managing, moderating, organizing and bridging its life-giving forces with a physical host is a complete wonder.

When issues are complex enough, there is no need to complicate our solutions.

In particular, we must not complicate our solutions by complicating our language. Vague spiritual jargon should not obfuscate what is already complex and mysterious.

Because humanity's quest to delve into spiritual mysteries is a complex subject, and because a lack in our spiritual language has lead to gross misunderstandings and, on occasion, gross errors, in this series, four volumes are required to adequately cover the bare minimum on the topic so as to ensure comprehensive (means cover all bases) and cohesive (means an union of diverse parts) coverage without forsaking our spiritual currency—for all of humanity (means every single person regardless of religious, socio-economic, political and/or national alliance).

My deliberate use of linguistic hiccups to break up an intentionally complex sentence above mirrors the labyrinth inherent in the topic. I encourage us not to kill the bearer of the message, as has been done on numerous occasions by previous generations before us.

Chapter 56.

Fact: Gather / Truth: Surrender

We gather facts. We surrender to truth.

Fact: Life comes with no guarantees.

Truth: Given that no mortal can offer a fail-safe guarantee in life, we may as well surrender to this truth and get on with living.

Fact: Life does not comes with a clear set of directions.

Truth: Given that no mortal has the definitive, complete and authentic set of instructions for life, we may as well surrender to this truth and get on with living our lives as best as we are able.

Fact: The date and time of a person's birth and death can be factually verified.

Truth: How intimately a person is graced by Spirit can only be truthfully known by the actual participant who is bound by the spiritual contract.

Fact: Justice can only prevail when facts are accurately presented.

Truth: Our judicial system is not immune to unjust manipulation by unconscionable lawyers.

Can and does the system make mistakes and fail our best social intentions? Yes. In light of these facts and truths, do we give up our quest for justice? No.

Fact: Southern California is overdeveloped and over-populated.

Truth: Seasonal fires are nature's way to cleanse, recycle and renew life.

Must there exist a cause-and-effect relationship between this fact and this truth? No. Could there exist a cause-and-effect relationship? Perhaps. Should we allow an exploration into the prevention of forest fires to mystify us? No.

Fact: A mysterious and energizing force imbues us with life.

Truth: Doctors do not literally possess life-sustaining powers. Doctors can only facilitate the life-giving nature of this force. Should we give this special force an obscure label and mystify entire generations of humanity? If our answer is "no", then how do we factually and truthfully account for Spirit's cultural presence, time and again, throughout human history?

Why do spiritual jargons seem to create an "is it a fact-or-truth" confusion in our cultural psyche?

Facts do not lie.

Truth, as painful and hard to come by sometimes, do not lie, either.

Just because a fact can be verified millions of times does not make it a truth.

Factually, the millions of Jews who were sacrificed by Hitler does not make ethnic cleansing an ethical truth.

In politics, majority rule may be a reliable fact, but when it comes to spiritual quest, the voice of one can truthfully empower billions.

Fact: Unlike insects, ordinary human vision is not synchronized for simultaneous telescopic and microscopic seeing. Truth: Spiritual exploration requires us to develop both our telescopic and microscopic viewing lenses so that we acquire the mental perspective to know the forest from the trees.

On a more comical note, Gordon Ramsey is the celebrity chef featured on "Hell's Kitchen". Truth: Hell's Kitchen does not literally stand for satan's dietary dispensary. Its viewing public does not feel compelled to dig deeply into their guts looking for evangelical truth just because the title of the reality TV show happens to have a skewed biblical reference.

There are countless other examples.

When it comes to spiritual truth, the requirement that factually verifiable data and events take concrete form may not *ever* be possible.

However, the methodology for exploring spiritual truths *must be systematic* because "mysterious" is not a factually valid cause to perpetuate secrets or hidden treasures.

Systematic means well structured and organized. And in truth, systematic need not imply scientific.

And as much as we may wish truths to take on the appearance of facts, we ought not presume that spiritual mysteries can *only* be truthfully known and factually disclosed "to the rest of us" by a few privileged individuals.

Truth, like the word "law", stands for the most profound, sacred, magnificent and awe-inspiring belief we hold in the most precious reaches of our hearts and souls.

Let us not forget that spiritual truths survive the test of time, regardless of the innumerable spiritual trends which may have risen to the top of popularity polls at any one given time throughout humanity's most triumphant cultures.

A systematic approach ensures a comprehensive gathering of factual data that can literally yield a more probable outcome of truthful disclosure, resolution and recovery of spiritual truths. Because for all intents and purposes, spiritual truths will probably always be subjective and inconclusive; and they may, therefore, appear factually open-ended. These four volumes are, truthfully, a humble beginning.

A presumption of truth is humanity's spiritual rite of passage.

Chapter 57.

Minutiae

There are the innumerable minute details of ordinary life. Many of them unnecessarily clutter our lives. A few of them, like breathing, are of such paramount importance; we rely on them to keep us alive.

Our cultural tendency to mentally dissect everything apart, examine the isolated details, and intellectually vacuum seal even our most sacred and mystifying features prevents us from living life in context, balance and harmony from our hearts.

Thirdly, there are the incredible array of vital details that Spirit must manage as it goes about the business of animating us with life.

Where doth the mundane and sacred meet?

For starters, let us start with some basics:

Exactly how does Spirit "come" to us?

Does it fly? Is it capable of flight? If so, how does it fly?

Does it have wings? Perhaps our archetypal allusions to heavenly "angels" and magical "fairies" originate from Spirit's wings of inspiration (title of volume two in this series)?

Why does Spirit bother to "appear" on the physical dimension?

What is "in it" for Spirit?

What does it "get" by participating in life?

Once it "arrives", "exactly" how does Spirit "align" itself within the form of its physical host?

Does Spirit "feel", as we do?

Does Spirit have "emotions"? If so, which ones?

Those of us who are not intimately connected with our humanity, does it make Spirit's job of animating us with life virtually impossible?

Does Spirit become frustrated or irritated with us?

How does Spirit "communicate" its dissatisfactions and vent its complaints?

Can we hear and/or know its "voice" of disgruntled dismay?

What about the laws of physics?

Do the laws of physics apply to Spirit's comings and goings?

This other "place" that Spirit comes from, "where" exactly is it?

Can we think of this "world" as Spirit's home or is it just a sort of temporary resting place?

Is Spirit a thrill-seeker of new adventures?

If so, does Spirit take a "mandatory rest stop" at this "other" place before it embarks on its next "flight"?

For how long must Spirit "rest"?

Does "time" operate differently "there" or does time operate much as we know it here?

If, in all likelihood, Spirit is on a different "time schedule", how does it tell "past" from "present" and "future" time?

Can the same Spirit "cohabit" different bodies "during the same durations" in "relative" time?

Can the physical cohabitations occur, for example, in two or more distant galaxies across opposites sides of the expanding universe?

Does Spirit only "visit" Earth?

Does Spirit "regularly" visit other star systems?

Are its visits "exclusively reserved" for this and only this planet?

How do other types of beings, for example, a dog, cat, tree, rock or, even possibly an extraterrestrial being like U2-384, explore their mysterious relationships with Spirit?

By what mode(s) of "communication, expression, language or dialogue" does Spirit and these other forms of life make their "feelings, thoughts and desires" mutually known to one another, given that dogs, cats, trees, rocks and ETs do not "speak" as humans do?

What "happens" right before we die?

What happens to Spirit after the physical body has "died"?

How does Spirit "separate" itself or "leave" the body that has been its "host"?

What happens to Spirit's "memories" of a lifetime?

Are the memories "recorded" or "imprinted" somehow for Spirit's future reference or recall?

What happens should there be an unforeseeable "accident" before, during or after the physical "alignment" process with its host?

Could these aligning "accident" leave permanent "scars", marks or residues with the physical body, for example, in the existing human host or conceivably in its "next" host?

Must the "blemish" be physical?

Could such a scar be mental, psychic, emotional and/or spiritual?

What is "everlasting" life?

What do we mean by "enlightenment"?

What do we mean by "incarnation"?

What is "re" incarnation, if we have difficulty explaining what a one-time incarnation is?

Is Spirit concerned with "finding out" the purpose of life?

If it is true that some of us are continually "searching" for "meaning in our lives", then could the same be said about Spirit?

Is it within Spirit's nature to continually search for meaning in its "life"—whatever life might be for a Spirit?

To "find" purpose, must Spirit "remember" what it has "learned" "previously"?

Is it the purpose of its many exciting adventures and trips teaching Spirit about its divine purpose?

In Spirit's "view", what does "divine" stand for?

Are the questions important or valid to the exploration?

How does "it" all work?

A minutia of basic questions such as these can easily fill an entire volume.

How do we use our language to clearly, precisely, factually and concretely capture these minute details? Perhaps before any of us venture to give our "definitive" answers, we ought to cover our bases by asking enough detailed questions—without bias or prejudice.

As far as Spirit is concerned, it is innately able to tolerate, manage and organize all sorts of minutiae.

If Spirit could speak, it may use its resounding voice to tell us:

"Not to bother with minutiae.
Answers to my mysteries will not
be hidden in the teeny-weeny wafers of earthly trifles.
I, Spirit, do not like to be bothered
by mundane details and in particular,
the innumerable inconsequential minutiae
associated with modern life. You, humans,
micromanage and multitask.
Yet, you cannot seem to grapple with
how minutiae inundate and clutter
your already complex lives."

Are we not distracted by enough details that there is no need to bring them into our personal reflections on the mysteries of Spirit?

Very simply, you must, without a doubt, peer deeply into your heart *in order to truthfully answer* each and every one of the above questions, plus more.

Chapter 58 .

The Contract

In our lives, we are all bound, in one way or another, by the many contracts we must honor.

For example, in the covenant of marriage; our informal arrangements about who serves as the financial provider in the family; who actually writes the checks to pay the bills; who rewards or disciplines the kids, and not to mention in the areas of work, friendship and love.

We can become so inundated by the many legally binding contracts we must honor in our lives that many of us forget we are each a holder of a spiritual contract.

This contract is between self, Spirit and soul.

It is a binding contract regardless of our age or status in life.

This is not a contract we sign with anyone else. Although we may not have put ink to paper and signed on the dotted line, this contact is stronger, more binding and power than any formalized, written contract.

The minutiae of terms named in this unspoken, unwritten and invisible-to-our-ordinary-senses contract is what we must navigate in life.

As we awaken to the terms named in the spiritual contract, we also realize our true purpose in life.

An inability to decipher the terms named causes us to feel uprooted and lost in life.

The Game of Life

Read on and you may find yourself flexing your telescopic and microscopic viewing lense, instead of tunneling through an egocentric worm's-eye view.

Act 11.

Universal Playing Field

The stage for play is the Universe.

Chapter 59.

Equal Opportunity

In matters of Spirit, every one is afforded the *same equal opportunity* to reflect on and explore its many mysteries. Furthermore, all are welcome to *participate* as equals.

This brand of equal opportunity is unparalleled in the human condition because it grants special privileges to no one particular person.

One's age, gender, breeding, race, ethnicity, level of education and even the time period lived in, whether long ago, contemporary or decades of generations later, do not target, favor or exclude anyone from embarking on a spiritual quest.

We are each granted equal opportunity to cultivate those skills which we would want to acquire for such a quest.

Equal opportunity, however, does not automatically translate into equal participation.

If equal participation were ubiquitous, it would not take a bulldozer to coax and convince a great majority of us to pay attention and act in consort with our spirits.

We are each granted equal responsibility to motivate, engage and personally participate. Because not only are we welcomed to participate as equals, but all must participate in one-way or another.

This egalitarian gesture spares no one. At some time in each person's life and, in particular in the face of crises, traumas or untimely fatalities, we are forced by life's circumstances to become intimately engaged.

Reality being what it is, perhaps Spirit would have been more prudent to afford us equal participation before gifting us with equal opportunity.

The opportunity is a tribute to the magnanimous spirit of a universe that demonstrate its unconditional trust in us without requiring us to do any thing besides being alive.

That an equal opportunity is universally made available and granted to each of us is a testament to the generosity and incredible leap of faith which grace human spirits.

Every one of us in a human form is not only given the same equal opportunity but the offer is given in a true spirit of independence.

This insight may beseech us to take more notice of the uniqueness of the quest which does not make one person any better or worse equipped than an other.

To be the recipient of such an egalitarian and generous privilege is to be given an invaluable gift.

An occasional small token of our gratitude for the egalitarian nature of the opportunity would be well placed and appreciated by the energy force which animates us with life.

The reality is that, in the actual living of our lives, few people make an effort to take the time out: first, to realize that life is an equal opportunity employer; and secondly, to express gratitude for this amazing gesture of equality.

Make good use of it.

Chapter 60.

Taking Form

If Spirit existed exclusively as a separate, invisible force of energy from our existence, it would remain just that. We would not need to engage ourselves with Spirit's mysterious comings and going nor would we need to have unending discussions about Spirit and its mysteries.

Given that, for us, Spirit does not exist in isolation from matter. Whether by consensus, default or the very nature of its essence, Spirit must align with our physical bodies.

That Spirit must infuse itself with form is a condition dictated by life. This paramount and steadfast rule can neither be violated by Spirit nor its human host.

Spirit may view the taking of human form as an obligation or it may view it as embarking on an exciting adventure.

If Spirit were able to speak to us, it might feel inclined to vent and complain about the nature of the physical beast. After all, our body is exceedingly fragile, prone to breakage and weak in its construction.

Perhaps Spirit considers itself quite a bit above menial tasks, such as our heart's nonstop actions of pumping blood; our gut's continual demand to be fed; our bowels having to store and discharge putrid waste; our sexual organs' insatiable drive to procreate, as well as many other physiological examples.

Perhaps Spirit feels indignant that it must stoop to such baseness.

Perhaps being the invisible energy force that it is, Spirit would rather float, drift and hover near the vicinity of its physical host without having to literally partake in any of the host's terrestrial misfortunes, diseases, sufferings and miseries.

In any case, when it melds with Earth's creatures, the physical constraints Spirit inevitably experience must hamper its customarily effervescent style.

Spirit, however, could take the opposite perspective. It may come to realize and appreciate its having to animate a living body. Spirit may enjoy the many adventures that combining with a human host adds to its education and missions in life—whatever these may be for Spirit.

It is only in the taking of form that insights into the secretive nature of life will be revealed—to us, as well as to Spirit.

This angle is worth exploring.

When it comes to spiritual exploration, one is permitted, if not mandated by inspiration, to dream beyond the stars and back.

In the game of life, the playing field is the universe.

The taking of human form may be one way in which Spirit gains entry into the playing field of life. In all due consideration, beside the human form, there must be many other forms in the universe for Spirit to choose from. Given the laws of physics, however, we cannot formally attest to what manifests elsewhere in the universe, as Spirit follows its preordained imperative to take form.

If Spirit could speak, what fantastic tales it would tell us. Many of these sagas must remain a mystery to us here on Earth. After all, not only are there the multitude of diverse life forms, of this planet but, from the perspective of Spirit, of the entirety of the universe.

At the very least, we can appreciate that Spirit must exhale a huge sigh of relief when the field of its animation is expanded to include the whole universe instead of merely on Earth.

In this spiritual playing field, creative lenience and tolerance is afforded to all. After all, imagine the creative feats that is required of Spirit as it sustains us with life.

Carry on, Spirit.

Chapter 61.

Body, Mind, Heart, Spirit

In taking form, each of us is granted a body.
Each of us possesses a mind.
Without a heart, both mechanical and poetic, we would not be exactly human.

Just as every human being is endowed with a body, mind and heart, by the same token, spirit graces every human being.

A primary focus for these four volumes is Spirit's intimate relationships with the human host.

As we go about our everyday routines, we often lose sight that the game requires our body, mind, heart and spirit to coexist within the close confines and finite spaces bound by our skin. And furthermore, that in their functions, they must be as intimately connected as Siamese "quadruplets". Not one single precious brain cell expends energy to "figure out" the incontrovertible connection that naturally exists between body, mind, heart and spirit.

In our hearts of hearts, who would not want to be healthy and fit in body; cognizant and aware in mind; loved and loving in heart; and ultimately, live life to the fullest, in every sense?

For each of us to be equally endowed with the faculties of body, mind, heart and spirit equalizes the playing field. With them, each of us begin life at the same starting point. No one has an added advantages or is disadvantaged over another human being.

The extent to which these faculties are cultivated and developed, however, is left entirely up to each person's free will.

Why some of us seek to develop, mature and advance in one aspect, few aspects, all aspects or none at all is a mystery.

When body, mind, heart and spirit work in balance as an united front, the game of life can be joyfully played to the fullest.

We can agree that all of earth's creatures are endowed with a body, heart and, depending on your existential view, spirit. However, we are unique among earth's creatures for our capacity to appreciate the value of a *unified* body, mind, heart and spirit.

To be gifted with all four aspects and also graced with our conscious capacity to observe, explore and recount the subtle, yet dynamic, interactions and interplay of body, mind, heart and spirit is a most ingenious feat of creation.

God bless you.

Chapter 62 .

Inviolable Union

The union of body, mind, heart and spirit is further strengthened by our inviolable connection to soul.

The codes to the mysterious genealogy between Spirit and soul may be one of most baffling to the human intellect—in so as much as we would like to think of ourselves, as intelligent, animated survival machines.

Simply put: Spirit and soul are inseparable.

Our linguistic blurring of their meanings may be a crude cultural inference of this inviolable union.

Soul, or essence, exists as one of the greatest and grandest mysteries of the universe.

By its inviolable union with soul, mortal life or death does not figure into Spirit's existence, survival, mystery or essence.

Soul's essence pervades the universe.

Soul's essence goes beyond merely the body, mind, heart and spirit.

For human beings, our hearts and spirits are the outsourcing of soul's essence.

Our bodies, minds, hearts and spirits do not, and cannot, exist separately from soul's essence.

The logical parts of our minds may be compelled to decode and give rational solutions.

Yet, we know "the true nature of essence" without a smidgeon of doubt. Our hearts and spirits deeply know that we must surrender to the inherent truth of the union—even though soul's essence will probably always evade our rational understanding.

Perhaps one reason Spirit bothers to take a human form may be so we would realize the inviolable bond of our union with soul.

Although it is virtually impossible for us to demonstrate beyond a shadow of doubt the tangible properties and characteristics of soul, let alone grasp its mysterious nature, most of us believe, with resounding personal conviction that, for lack of a better term, soul's essence must "somehow" exist in every region and corner of the cosmos.

Our hearts and spirits know how to feel at peace living with a perpetual mystery that may never reveal its secrets to us.

Such is the inviolable union between humanity and soul.

Chapter 63.

Another World

Spirit comes to us from another world.

The other world (realm, dimension, plane and any other celestial terms for it) is where soul permanently resides. Soul calls this "place" its home. To transition from living to beyond living is to return us to our eternal home. This eternal home exists in a world so vastly different from ours that it takes the exquisite words of poets, visionaries, mystics and prophets to sing its praise.

Although varying civilizations and cultures over the millennia:

Have had different names for it.

Given elaborate descriptions of it.

And told us what we needed to do in life in order to enjoy our eternal sojourn there after death. If a permanent resident visa were conditionally offered to this other world, every single one of us would undoubtedly accept the generous offer.

While alive, we cannot concretely demonstrate or attest to the origins of Spirit, soul and their otherworldly home. After its disengagement from the physical body, we choose to believe that Spirit rejoins soul's essence in the other world.

The other side is mysterious and inaccessible. Its secrets are hidden. As such, we cannot leave it alone. It is our spiritual nature to be mystified by it.

The physical laws of nature will mostly likely not pertain or be applicable there. Weight, mass, matter, location, geography and space operate differently. Any conversations about it will surely defy our current knowledge of physical laws.

Time, for example, operates differently. It may not be the ordinary keeping of time that we do with our clocks and watches. The perceptual chronicle of past, present and future may blur, intersect or become entirely random. Suffice it to say that beyond mere speculations, none of us really knows or can know for certain.

Try as we might, entry into this other world is not penetrable or permissible by the living.

If Spirit could speak, it might offer helpful clues about the other world. But since it cannot, we will continue to blunder along, hoping that some of our speculations are at least on mark.

Because time and space take on drastically different character from what we know here on Earth, it *is* conceivable that entirely different lifetimes might interweave a complicated web of simultaneous coexistence within the span of what we ordinarily perceive to be a blink in time.

Where does that leave us? Mystified, for sure.

A view into the other world need not be literally factual. More often than not, such a view is defended mystically rather than rationally.

Furthermore, since essence is pervasive throughout, access to the other world is made equally available for all to explore. This situation affords everyone an opportunity to be an authority on the subject matter.

Yet, none possesses the capacity to proof beyond a shadow of a doubt whether their view might be tarnished by the inadequacies of our earthly perceptions or whether essence is actively responsible for the direct transference of accurate spiritual information.

Men and women with the capacity to simultaneously embrace incorporeal dimensions and our current understanding of physical laws can do so without appearing insane because they are mentally, psychically and spiritually mature enough to realize the difference between a mystery and a delusion.

The singularity of a spatial and temporal enigma, again,

equalizes the playing field for every participant in the game of life and death.

As spirits, we may compare notes when we see one another on the other side.

See you on the other side.

Chapter 64.

Laws

There are nature's laws. These are the cardinal laws of the universe. Without them, everything we know on Earth, the Milky Way and beyond would not exist in their present form and state.

Then, there are man-made laws. These are mankind's humble attempts to formulate natural laws.

If Spirit could speak, perhaps it would tell all of humanity to:

> "Learn the rules;
> understand the rules;
> follow the rules;
> and, finally, play by the rule."

This simple, and far from mysterious, formula helps humanity to grow, develop and mature spiritually.

We must remind ourselves that the natural world does not stop at the doorsteps of our terrestrial biosphere. Its boundaries extend to the billions of stars that make up the known universe. Although the universe does not literally reach infinity, to our minds, it may just as well.

In our valiant efforts to empower the minds and spirits of mankind, we ought not bastardize universal laws by our packaging, marketing and commercializing of them.

Context must accurately reflect nature, rather than man-made ideas.

Repeat: do not distort nature's laws.

Natural laws, such as the law of attractive forces, are quite specific in their universal effects. Humanity's misappropriations shall have no lasting effects because universal laws will simply manifest into reality that which is accurate and true.

Secondly, do not shroud what may appear mysterious and unknowable by ordinary human means behind a veil of secrecy, secret societies and privileged Initiates.

The best of us will want to refrain from codifying laws which violate nature's laws.

This goes for spiritual laws as well.

One prevailing rule being: life ultimately disregards our theories or laws regarding her dominion.

Life does not hold lengthy discourse over cause and effect.

Humanity does. Our laws governing cause and effect appease our existential fear of the unknown forces of life.

Cosmology views how the universe is put together. Therefore, all spiritual explorations must also presuppose, and graciously accept without our egos' interferences, an underlying cosmological view that strengthens our intimate contact with all which exists in the universe.

Should there ever be a contest, Mother Nature will always triumph. Nature has very expedient and powerful ways of rectifying misrepresentations of her laws. Furthermore, let us not forget that her gauge of time is vastly more relative than humanity's millions of years on this terrestrial planet.

Regardless of the tenacity of human willpower, man-made laws must stay true to the laws of nature and the universe. Otherwise, mankind will pay the consequences for our misappropriations. The laws that govern Spirit, and our crude adaptations of these laws, are no exception.

Caveat emptor.

Stage 5 .

Our Modern Dilemmas

Act 12 .

Entertaining Twists

*Bizarre money aberrations
of the ET sort.*

Chapter 65.

Psycho Emotional, Not Spiritual

Lost, Survivor, The Amazing Race, The Moment of Truth, Deal or No Deal, Are You Smarter Than a Fifth Grader, Eli Stone, Heroes, Medium, Ghost Whisperer, Raising Daisies, Journeyman, New Amsterdam, The Love Guru, Heaven Almighty, Meeting Joe Black, Phenomena, Signs, The Sixth Sense, Music of the Heart, Step Up 1 & 2, Fool's Gold, Bedazzled, Vantage Point, The War of the Worlds. Are these mythic metaphors for the game of life and, therefore, programmed to help us intimately contact Spirit?

As TV shows and Hollywood movie titles, they are a testament of art imitating life or, more accurately, entertainment art imitating life. They claim to be the most watched TV shows and box office successes because we get a kick out of seeing our most twisted psychodramas played out on the big screen.

I wonder, though, how many of their viewers actually take in the deeper spiritual lessons on accountability and vulnerability (The Moment of Truth); hope and optimism (Deal or No Deal); and memory and recall (Are You Smarter than a Fifth Grader?).

Children who are fed a constant diet of chocolate grow up with a craving for chocolates. When we are fed a constant diet of psychodramas, we end up craving psychodramas. Neither diet is good for the body or soul (mind).

Twists may be fine on television and in the movies but not in real life.

Psychodramas twist our psyches and minds.

They play to the weakest link of human nature. They bait us by drawing us in. We become victims to our own psychic weakness for surprise endings, wit and cheap thrills.

When we cannot tell the difference between real life and make-believe, we should not expect our spiritual compass to know the difference, either.

It goes back to an elaborate interweaving of our multiple energy pathways. Point in fact: given that the same set of psyche, emotions, mind, body and spiritual compass must belong to the same human host, common sense tells us that we cannot expect one channel to be awakened, while other channels are sound asleep.

If only all of us were fortunate enough to be psychoemotionally mature as well as mentally astute, then perhaps we would know the difference between a fictional depiction and a real live event.

When our emotional and psychical engagement is controlled by outside forces with ulterior motives, then we have lost control over our own spiritual destiny.

An intimate contact with Spirit helps us authentically make spiritual choices in life rather than fall for commercialized spirituality.

Chapter 66.

Spin Masters, Ad Gurus and Business as Usual

This section speaks to a conflict of interest between Big Business and spirituality. Truthfully, there is no way around the dilemma.

Momentum, money and media are the 3 M's of modern commerce.

The law of supply and demand is pretty straightforward. The entertainment industry is built on an exchange of fun and pleasure for money. The business formula is a simple one: human beings are, by and large, unassuming creatures. Given a choice, most of us would choose pleasure over pain. Entertainment brings us pleasure. Spirituality lifts our spirits and is therefore pleasurable.

Combine spirituality with entertainment; throw in some advertising, marketing and sophisticated packaging and presentation; a couple of glamorous celebrity eye candies; and there is a fail-safe business plan for making lots of money—for everyone concerned.

Spirituality as a commodity has not escaped the attention of Big Business. Just follow the ripple effect in the form of a money trail, from the gurus, yogis, televangelist preachers, publicists, advertisers, Hollywood, television, magazines, books, radio stations and everyone in between to make it all happen—and, of course, the end consumers.

The job requirements of spin masters and ad gurus are dictated by the tenets of commerce. They must perform. They must sell products. In business, the bottom line is earnings. When they deliver the goods, they are generously rewarded. As such, they know more about making a presentation using multiple angles than the rest of us. They have refined ad campaigns, packaging, public relations and marketing into an extraordinarily sophisticated art form.

Take a count the next time you have the television switched on from 7-11 PM. In any given three-hour block of prime-time airtime, we are bound to hear the word "twist" on average two to three times every night.

Have you noticed? Have you wondered, "what is up with that"? Nowadays, every time I hear the word "twist" on TV, I cringe.

The business of telling us what we desire in life is a billion dollar industry. If we operated according to the entertainment industry's version of supply and demand, they would seduce us into believing we are dying to be twisted by jaw-dropping, on the edge-of-your-seat suspense and intrigue. Entertaining twists, like designer brands, happens to be one of the industry's favorite sidearms.

When he is not studying coins, our resident alien anthropologist, may draw the conclusion from his observations that earthlings are a group of creatures who worship mental and psychic contortionists.

Entertaining twists play on our emotions. As an example, had I wanted a dramatic accent here, I could have added a witty twist—"is it an extraterrestrial or entertaining twist?"—about ET's, U2-384 and his numismatist views. Particularly in view of the fact that where he comes from, they know little about commercial value. But what would be the point, besides indulge in my egotistical whims, imitate entertaining twists or pat my own back with the hope that my readers would find me clever? In which case, would I be smarter than a fifth grader or would I fail in my moment of truth because I made a commercial deal with an alien being who knows zilch about commerce?

Those of us who are intimately familiar with the human psyche realize that it can be the most wonderfully twisted part of our human nature. Then, there are the odd twists of fate where an enormous tragedy turns into extraordinary gifts of life. But for the sake of god, how many different ways are there to twist a sour lemon?

By comparison, the law of supply and demand for life is far simpler: live or die. In life, the bottom line is survival. In order for there to be business earnings, one must be alive.

It is wise to assume that we get only one chance in life. And as much as the ad gurus and spin masters of commerce may introduce new twists, entertainment cannot put a dent in this existential tag line.

In our spiritual quest, we would not want to be naive. The fact is: the topic of spirituality is not immune to the widespread influence of Big Business.

Let me be clear: Mass media is not an evil that must be eradicated so that it does not corrupt humanity with its decadent ways. I would simply like to point out that, although we are continually bombarded by commerce, we seldom take a moment to seriously reflect on the residual effects it may have over spiritual exploration.

No one wants to be seduced by misguided paths of seductive spiritual conquests. The extreme twists we are willing to make in order to buy and sell has assumed such extraordinarily common place in our lives, we seldom question their spiritual implications

Entertaining twists is the *game* inside the game—of life.

It is not my intention to introduce a twist here.

Life simply is not a commodity that can be cleverly packaged, marketed and sold to whomever can afford to buy it. Nor should it be.

Our humanity is not a commodity. Nor is spirituality.

How would we like it if the spirit that animates us with

life energy takes a business-as-usual attitude in how it keeps us alive?

Would you desire that from your personal spirit?

We should not assume Spirit's view in this matter to be self-evident. If Spirit could have a view—which it most certainly must—Spirit would not view the business of life as a commodity. Neither should we.

I implore us to put entertaining twists in the context of our spiritual lives.

Genuinely substantive exploration into our spiritual nature *must not* introduce twists.

If the existential weight of the previous sentence does not hit each one of us squarely between the eyes like a ton of bricks, our resignation confirms how much many of us take entertaining twists for granted.

Because given a choice, would you really choose an entertaining twist over spiritual truth?

We have a choice.

We must prudently exercise our choice in life.

The choice requires perspective.

We gain perspective when we stop twisting our insatiable hunger to be gratified emotionally by outside resources and, instead, back the power triad of self-spirit-soul. We must listen to our common sense and gut instinct. Spiritual aptitude requires us to develop an authentic balance between the multiple channels of our physical, mental, emotional, psychological, spiritual and existential energy pathways.

A spirit of charity must be balanced with a spirit of enterprise.

Chapter 67.

Compelling Stories

Human beings are social animals. One way we share social interactions is by our talking to one another. By our talking we feel more connected and intimate with one another. Beside, our talking entertains us.

Storytelling is humanity's oldest form of entertainment. We love our storytelling.

As our ancestors sat under the starlit skies and huddled around a bonfire, they amused themselves by telling each other stories. Each time a story is retold, the details are embellished and slightly altered to sustain the listeners' interest with its many repetition. We have inherited this love.

Many of us spend countless hours repeating our stories over and over again. We feel compelled to tell our biographical histories to others. Like our stargazing ancestors, we feel soothed and understood when we pour our hearts out to each other.

The telling of stories, however, can turn one of humanity's favorite pastimes into an obsessive compulsion.

When we talk about something, we are not living and being. We are more concerned with talking about it.

Talking "about" is an action that immediately pulls us away from having an intimate contact with Spirit and ourselves, because "about" must refer to something outside oneself.

We do not realize we have objectified our lives and ourselves.

Those of us who hold on to our stories as if our survival depended on them are cheating ourselves of living an authentic life.

We are so consumed by the telling and retelling of our stories; we've lost all sight of what is truly important in life. Instead of really getting down to the serious business of living, we delude ourselves to believe that having an attentive audience validates our existence.

Spare me the drama.

Life is not a story.

Besides, a life's stories cannot be told if it is not first lived.

And although our stories may be a way for us to celebrate the grace of Spirit, we cannot contact Spirit by talking alone.

Just as the background white noise that fills many of our cars, homes and shopping malls, a great deal of our talking distracts us from fully contacting Spirit.

An over-reliance on our storytelling distances us from Spirit because humanities' collective voice gets caught up by fairy tales and fantasies, rather than express a genuine intimacy with life.

For those of us looking for more in life, realize that—to be consumed by our stories, either in our telling or viewing of them—is to waste our precious vital life energies.

The consequence of which is an incapacity to hear and commune with Spirit.

Spirit does not tolerate being disposed of.

There is a saying: a person is as good as his or her word.

Let your own stories of discovery, recovery, courage, purpose and intimate contact inspire you. The topic of inspiration will be covered in more detail in Volume II, *Wings of Inspiration*.

Chapter 68

Headlines, Snapshots and Voyeuristic Limelight

On January 13, 2008, "60 Minutes" featured an Anderson Cooper piece on the systematic rape of nearly four million East Congolese women by their own militia. The atrocities are so heinous and dehumanizing that to see it described in print would sicken us.

Sitting in the comforts of our cozy homes, to know that there are parts of the world where sex is used as a weapon. Where family members are forced to witness, and sometimes take part in, gang rapes. Where the mutilation of female genitalia by bayonets and beer bottles is a show of force and power. And where women have simply given up living.

We as a society have got to wonder why the latest celebrity child custody battles, marriage breakups, drug overdoses and DUI mug shots consume more of our media airtime than atrocities against humanity?

Certainly, headlines inform us about the world we live in and a picture can be worth a thousand words. To use the power of media to teach and inspire millions of people worldwide is wonderful. That is not what this is about.

We have turned into a culture of voyeurs. With the instant click of a camera phone, we can all be documentary journalists.

Voyeurs expend their mental and psychic energies viewing other people's lives versus living their own. By watching the lives of others from the outside, a voyeur's psychic pathology remains anonymous and uninvolved. Voyeurs get a thrill out of their clandestine viewings, rather than intimately connect in their own lives.

Commerce makes it its business to sell us sensational headlines, instant snapshots and compelling stories. Compelling stories sell because, the more compelling the story, the more it hooks us with its entertainment value. This would be fine if, like young children, all we wanted out of life was a constant supply of play—on words.

Media hype hooks us by creating a whirlwind of emotions. The idea is to circumvent our reason and sound judgment. There are the quick fixes; timesaving tricks; fast, easy and simple conveniences; revolving line of credit; and layaway plans. Not happy on the inside, in an instant, get an extreme makeover on the outside.

"That ought to take care of all our problems."

Many of us choose to be seduced by these taunting messages.

The presence of headlines and snapshots in the media limelight should not shamefully seduce our egos into consuming a plethora of glamour and hype.

Bulletin headlines and journalistic snapshots, however informative they may be, do not represent real life. Real life does not fit neatly on a 2-dimensional medium.

In the context of each of our biographical histories, newsworthy events and captivating images are literally frozen moments in time.

Truthfully, reality happens over an entire lifetime which spans countless life events and distinct montages.

The entertainment industry has turned compelling storytelling into a mega blockbuster of a business tycoon.

Just because we see something in print or on celluloid does not mean it is life enhancing.

And just because we do not see something in print or on celluloid does not mean that it is not newsworthy or, at the very least, worth a drop of our human compassion. Because just how *do* we twist snapshots of brutally raped, tribal African women into a commodity?

The answer is: we don't. And unfortunately, their stories stay out of the public eye.

We cannot look to market trends to steer us in our spiritual explorations.

Along with the carefully edited tabloid bleeps, memorable photographs and sensation media coverage, do we explicitly instruct our young people that the events they see and hear are isolated moments of an entire biographical history?

Given all of life's inevitable ups and downs, would our kids courageously live their lives from the honesty of their biographical achievements as well as failures?

Do our kids realize that of all the biographical histories of humanity, the story of their own life is the most compelling and newsworthy of all?

Would our children feature spotlights of themselves, even though no one else but their spirits are watching?

What are headlines, snapshots and media limelight really teaching our youngsters spiritually?

If as adults, we allow those compelling tales about the recovery of Spirits of others pull us out of our existential focus; what message is unwittingly coming across to our kids?

Are we getting these extremely important messages across?

When we are continually fed a steady diet of compelling stories, those of us who are not as intimately connected with our true identity may conclude that: only those people whose lives are continually on public display are worthy of media attention—and therefore attention from the rest of humanity.

If we do not offer our kids model examples, they will look to that which is made so prevalently available by our society.

As voyeurs, many of us share more intimacy with total strangers than with ourselves. Rather than inspiring ourselves by triumphantly living our own lives, we *are* covertly influencing our kids, imprinting future generations and leaving behind a legacy of mixed spiritual messages.

The case in point being again: how would our children learn true values in life but for what we put forth to them, especially when the adults among us are just as clueless?

If a snapshot were taken of each of us, the moment we took our first breath after gliding from our mothers' wombs, to the moment before our last breath on earth, and every microsecond in between—sound awake or asleep—"you" *are* as you have been and always will be.

These are the snapshots we ought to be concerned with. Not the ones we view on our airwaves.

"Who you are" may be three simple words. We seem to hear it voiced a lot in the media these days. But what do we really mean by them?

Spirit aches for us.

I implore us to put entertaining twists in the context of our spiritual life.

To exchange our intimate spiritual contact with a seductive tabloid that happened in the blink of an eye truthfully distorts reality.

Spirit views these twisted scenarios with great sadness, disappointment and longing.

In order to succeed in life, we must align with Spirit and focus our undivided spiritual attention for the entire span of a lifetime—and not just a few fleeting moments.

Chapter 69.

Hearsay

Words in our ears, hear. Words straight out our mouths, say. With nothing much substantive going on in between gives us the word *hearsay*.

Oral tradition is one of our most treasured rituals. We orally imitate what is around us. Usually, a third-party has passes on the information, rather than our actually having experienced the event firsthand. So-and-so said or did such-and-such. By virtue of it having been publicly laundered, "it" becomes fact.

Our oral imitations take form in popular culture. They become imbedded in our cultural consciousness. En masse, we accept these imitations as though they are self-evident truths. When in reality, many of them began as gossip, rumors and hearsay. Like a chain letter, these pop culture oral imitations duplicate, replicate, propagate and reproduce, almost seemingly of their own accord.

Take for example the law of attraction which has gained popularity in many spiritual circles. The popularized law of attraction tells us we attract what we want to us. In nature, the male of a species will be sexually attracted to the female. This kind of animalistic attraction has the feel of a strong "magnetic" impulse. And therefore in our casual conversations, attraction seems to be a fitting description.

Nearly 10.5 billion years before it came into print and eons into the future, a powerful force of the universe dictated that opposites attract and likes repel. An electron (negatively charged particle) and its oppositely charged particle, the proton, are *attracted* to one another. By the same principle, electrons repel electrons and protons repel protons.

The attractive force is the glue that binds the physical world—as we know it, not just here on Earth but of the entire universe. To extrapolate a powerful force that governs the behavior of galaxies, supernovas and subatomic particles for the purpose of advancing human potential is to apply the law in its original and unadulterated form.

A law of the universe is exactly that.

To arbitrarily pluck universal "laws" out of thin air for human consumption is inexcusable. Therefore, unless we possess the almighty power to *exclude* ourselves from universal forces that modulate powerful actions in the physical world, the same effect must therefore also apply for human thoughts.

Oral tradition is one of the oldest forms of information sharing. Before there was the printing press, facsimile, telecommunication and the Internet, we relied on oral tradition to pass on information. And as such, there is nothing wrong with it per se.

However, we ought not fall for, be seduced or succumb to indulgent or lazy dialogues that create more confusion than bring forth resolutions. Just because quasi-spiritual jargons are proclaimed widely and loudly, get tons of publicity and media attention, sound right or are seductively enticing does not mean they are spiritually true. The law of attraction is, unfortunately, based on hearsay passed on by authors who may be well meaning but who, apparently, must have flunked their second-grade physical science class.

For although sexual attraction serves to repopulate species of animals, primal magnetism is a base instinct. Those of us who are existentially mature know that the immediacy of a psychoemotional impulsive may be an indicator of pathological compulsions rather than martial compatibility.

If our intent is to empower humanity, at the very least, check the facts (of the physical, mental and psychological varieties) and take a careful look at the world we actually live in (of the physical, mental and psychological varieties) before venturing to introduce erroneous misconceptions that take pop culture years to rectify.

The correct and accurate terms are "to harmonize or attune" —as in the law of harmony or the law of attunement, rather than the "law of attraction".

Are we intending to empower ourselves by magnetically drawing to us the opposite of what we desire, or do we stay in tune with our desires by harmonizing our minds?

According to physical principles, to harmonize and attune is to bring into agreement or synchrony. Melodies that are in tune are harmonious. Whereas, as has already been pointed out, attraction magnetically draws the opposite charge.

Take a break from your mental chatter and digest what you have just read.

Correction: we want to harmonize in (rather than attract) positive thoughts. Opposites attract and likes repel; therefore, positive thoughts "attract" negative thoughts, and positive thinking "repels" positive thinking—not quite what we had in mind.

We want to harmonize in (rather than attract) financial abundance. Opposites attract and likes repel; therefore, financial abundance "attracts" financial impoverishment and destitution, and financial abundance "repels" wealth—not quite what we had in mind.

We want to harmonize in (rather than attract) health. Opposites attract and likes repel; therefore, health "attracts" sickness and disease, and health "repels" wellbeing—not quite what we had in mind.

We want to harmonize in (rather than attract) knowledge. Opposites attract and likes repel; therefore, knowledge "attracts" ignorance, and knowledge "repels" wisdom—not quite what we had in mind.

We want to harmonize in (rather than attract) spiritual truth. Opposites attract and likes repel; therefore, spiritual truth "attracts" spiritual lies, and spiritual truth "repels" true spirituality—not quite what we had in mind.

A misappropriation of the "law" of attractive forces has become so culturally ingrained that to see it accurately transcribed in print feels psychoemotionally incorrect.

Not to mention, it takes lots of words to right cultural errors.

By harmonizing and attuning, wonderful things just seem to spontaneously materialize, without our having to transform our heads into gigantic wobbling magnets.

Truly liberating spiritual lessons, tools, teachings, discoveries and conclusions are typically first met with social ridicule, suspicion and popular resistance. The "law of attraction" is only one of many examples throughout human civilization where our uses of "secretive" spiritual language meant for a few privileged and enlightened beings further mystifies the enigma rather than clear a path for the seekers of spiritual truths.

In hearsay, words goes into the ear and is verbally regurgitated—without much central processing by the white and gray matters located between our ears.

Our speaking and listening tools are set on autopilot.

The problem with hearsay is, as every master storyteller knows, by the time of its sixth repetition, the details of the original message would have been embellished, elaborated and altered beyond its original form. I predict that by the sixth repetition, someone will mistakenly accuse this section of the book for attacking positive thinking and personal fulfillment.

Our repetition of spiritual catch phrases have become automatic because the same economic cogwheels that replicate our tools and machines also produce a steady supply of spiritual hearsay.

We hear spiritually loaded words and catch phrases used, but do most of us, for example, truly understand "karma"? Yet, we hear it widely used.

Many of us casually offer to say "prayers" for total strangers, when we are not churchgoers, do not consider ourselves religious and have no idea how to say prayers for ourselves. By prayers, we simply mean we offer thoughts of sympathies for someone's perils and not necessarily that we are vocally transmitting a request which we have faith will be duly granted by a divine source.

Some of us load certain events with spiritual meaning. They are "sign" guiding us on a spiritual "path", to the extent that we cannot make even the simplest of life decisions.

These days, instead of politically correct, it is fashionable to be spiritually correct. Have you started talking to some folks only to find that they sound like a parody of their favorite spiritual mentor, teacher or author? We have all met our share of people who tell us they are spiritually inclined and have found their spiritual path in life. Yet, it is quickly apparent their spiritual repetitions, instead of sounding sincere, are a monotonous drone of empty words. Their word choices are all good, yet somehow they sound disingenuous. We can sense their lack of an intimate contact with Spirit. They are influenced more by hearsay than a genuinely personal quest for spiritual truth.

All twists aside, hearsay is the oldest form of publicity known to mankind. Novelty generates buzz. Buzz, regardless of its content, is good for business. Novelty, glamour and hype drive publicity. Publicity, of any kind, drives notoriety. Notoriety drives sales. Sales equal positive cash flow. Good advertisement generates a lot of buzz by getting lots of people talking about a hot new item.

Hearsay is a sophisticated form of the ancient art of gossip because it relies on us to pay lip service. It is safe to say that every one of us has been the brunt of idle gossip. Uncorroborated gossip taints personal character and integrity. Furthermore, it takes a lot of public relations to clear the mess up. Realize that every news-worthy tidbit, and many of the not so worthy stories, must pass through someone else's filter. Every instance of oral repetition must literally qualify as hearsay because, unless we personally are at the scene, we are being fed the news bulletin.

The same can be said of spiritual axioms based on hearsay.

Do not listen to everything you hear.

Moreover, do not believe everything you hear.

Self-help with a little bit of entertainment does not qualify as spirituality.

Hearsay is second-hand information and, as such, qualifies as gossip. We must not trust our intimate spiritual connection to hearsay, especially not the spiritually based enticements used by marketing firms to seduce our egos and subdue our common sense.

When it comes to matters concerning Spirit and its many mysteries, we would not want to rely on or trust our spiritual explorations to second-hand gossip—especially when someone else tells you they know more about your intimate connection with Spirit than you.

We must experience, explore and understand spiritual mysteries firsthand. Not doing so would amount to treating gossip as facts. Where Spirit is concerned, to treat gossip as fact amounts to spiritual ignorance.

Ignorance leads to a mental vacuum.

Act 13 .

The Games Most Commonly Played

Listen up. I have news for you.

Chapter 70.

Magic

Spirit does not use magic to render life.

Magic tricks fool our ordinary senses by its sophisticated use of illusions. Certainly, magic delights and entertains us.

Humanity finds magical causes for those extraordinary events which cannot be verified by ordinary means. There are parts of the world where indigenous tribesmen refuse to be photographed; because they believe the device "steals" their spirits. An ordinary camera is not technically capable of siphoning the gift of life into its black box. When a native touches the flat screen of a DVD player or cell phone with his fingers, he feels coldness rather than warm flesh. He believes the spirit of the person is either bewitched or has passed onto another dimension. Because how can someone whom he knows is physically halfway across the globe simultaneously appear on a flat screen? Flipping a switch to bring light into a darkened room is made possible by modern electricity and not divine enlightenment.

Some of us may laugh at these extreme examples.

Immature minds and psyches, however, are prone to magic tricks.

Descriptions of invisible phenomena are difficult to articulate. If we can't touch it, hold it, smell it, copy it, and have it stand still long enough so that we can at least get a physical "glimpse" of it, then how can we ever be sure that we are conversing about the same "thing"?

The gift of life is a miracle.

Spirit is no master of illusion.

As much as Spirit's miraculous ways fall outside ordinary physical laws, and therefore may forever defy our ordinary understanding, humanity's spiritual explanations ought to stay away from magic tricks and illusory myths. For the simple reason that when the psyche is deeply scarred and the heart deeply pained, our spirits are vulnerable to tricks of illusion.

Masters of illusion can be found in every profession, including the honorable one that counsels humanity on matters of Spirit. In many parts of the world, including modern western culture, magical beliefs in Spirit's mysterious ways still prevalently exist.

Spirituality backed by magic perpetuates a culture of ignorance.

Humanity's explanation of Spirit's life-giving feat must not resort to magic.

We know better because we are privileged by our education.

Any spiritual exploration must cultivate a balance between its teachings and our intrinsic spiritual common sense.

Spiritual explanations must pass the judgment of our common sense and gut instinct. For the simple fact that because Spirit resides within us, we can tap into the breadth of its knowledge and wisdom, when we choose to be intimately connected.

As we embark on a spiritual quest, our tendency to favor ignorance and avoidance rather than intimately contact with our gut instinct may be one of our biggest psychoemotional obstacles.

In which case, Spirit would have no recourse but feel deeply offended and disappointed by our gross misrepresentation of its wonders.

Chapter 71.

Perfection

The game of perfection seems to have infected a great many of us.

The game goes something like this: aspire to be perfect; when we attain perfection, then we will be rewarded with adoration and love—from others.

Women are particularly prone to the game of perfection. They have been conditioned to feel as though they are not good enough just as they are. Therefore, they must strive to be perfect; for then, they deserve to be loved. (For some reason, men tend towards idealism and women tend towards perfectionism.)

Perfection is an illusion.

An axiom of spiritual truth is: no human being can be perfect. Try as we might, human beings cannot be perfect. This reality is an inviolable rule of the game of life here on Earth. If we were, we would be god.

Imagine how it would work on this planet if there were nearly six and a half billion gods running around—each with our own versions of salvation, redemption, absolute benevolence and creation. Put into such an extreme context, the absurdity of the perfection game makes perfect common sense.

Survival for a perfectionist is dependent on a reality that is impossible to attain—a reality which does not exist in the world that we all know and live in.

Do we want to live to the end of our imperfect lives with

an anguish brought on by striving to be perfect? At which point, we realize that death must qualify as the most imperfect of all human traits because, in a perfect world, no one would die.

Interview a perfectionist. The distortions in self at the expense of a deluded ego and superego are heartbreaking.

Human beings who aim to manifest perfection are doomed to failure, because they are fighting against a preordained spiritual law.

Shattering the delusion may cause a few psychic upsets but, in the long run, can be lifesaving.

Imperfection is one of our sacred privileges. Turn these sound byte into a cultural mantra: human beings are created to be imperfect; to be human is to fully embrace our imperfect nature; and lastly, our wholehearted acceptance of our imperfections releases us from bondage.

Walking away from the game of perfection can bring an individual immediate peace of mind and calmness in spirit.

Let this be an open call to all the perfectionists out there: get a healthy reality check on life; or else, life will inevitably deliver a rude wake-up call and force perfectionists to take a good hard look at themselves.

Instead, seek a perfect marriage between self and Spirit.

Chapter 72.

Idealism

We turn our ideas into ideals. And then we wonder why we are not happy in life.

What ever happened to: just letting life happen?

Objectively observe what happens. Pause.

Then, analyze what happens—*in that order.* This life process keeps us grounded in concrete reality, rather than steep ourselves in conjectures that have nothing to do with real life.

Most people live their lives from the confined arenas of their thought processes. Rather than staying mentally alert and gauging our responses to each unique life circumstance, rigidly holding onto our ideals enables us to feel secure and comfortable in life.

We do not have to think for ourselves. Our superegos simply defer to our ideals.

Our living is not based on empirical observations but on idealized speculations.

Western culture favors idealism because we inherited a philosophical ideal from Plato, who is widely known as the father of idealism. The Golden Ratio, an ideal balance of geometric proportions, and platonic love are two ideals we attribute to this classical branch of Greek philosophy.

Ideals are commendable.

However, when ideals turn into mental perfections and supersede our intimate contact with humanity, existential problems arise.

Over time, our ideals turn into absolutes. Life is too dynamic and mercurial for mankind's tendency to favor absolutes.

An ideal: the ladies of the gentry constrict their midriffs with whalebones, secure their genitalia within plates of armor and bind their feet with cloth bandages to preserve an ideal of honor, chastity and beauty upheld by the cultural standards of the time. Not much thought was given to the dire health consequences.

An ideal: Egyptian royalties built architectural marvels and filled them with extraordinary riches. Ideally, they retained the same material privileges in the afterlife as they had been granted while alive. Not much thought was given to the countless slaves whose lives were needlessly sacrificed.

An ideal: Our ancestors had a fight with someone—over food, land, maidens, brawn, conquest, beliefs or just because they were plain bored. Hundred of years later, we still hate them. Ideally, we believe that if we eradicate every one of them; we will be rewarded by god for purifying our planet. We teach this to our children. And the cycle of ideal remains unbroken.

An ideal: the ethic cleansing of one race over another under the guise of racial purity by mass extermination in gaseous monstrosities of burial chambers. Not much thought was given to the atrocity, criminality and inhumanity of the acts.

An ideal: modern pirates hack off the dorsal fins of hundreds of sharks. They reap millions of dollars for the purportedly idealistic elixir and medicinal properties, while senselessly dumping cargo-loads of fin-less carcasses overboard to rot and die. Not much thought was given to the savagery, assault, pain and suffering inflicted on one of god's magnificent creatures.

An ideal: good, wholesome teenage girl do not have babies out of wedlock. To rid themselves of their accidental pregnancies, the newborns are dispassionately abandoned in dumpsters and public bathrooms as if they were trash. Not much thought was given to the marvel of life.

We take our idea of "what a husband should be"; set "it" in a mental mold and expect "husband" to perform to our ideal expectations, while rejecting the actual living person. While we are at it, let us expand the list to include: wife, parent, girl, boy, teenager, friend, best friend, marriage, love, happiness, security, faith, compassion, altruism, saving the planet, god and spirituality. We set them in mental molds and expect these aspects of life to perform to our ideal expectations.

There are hundreds of examples, large and small.

Ideal: follow and obey all rules and laws. We will be rewarded in kind. Life will not deal us its share of injustices. Real: Let us see what actually happens in life.

Ideal: push body beyond its physiological limits. Our conscious control of mind over body means we will excel in life. Real: let us see what actually happens to the body in the long run.

Ideal: be a pal and friend to our children. They will appreciate and love us. Real: let us see how they actually turn out in life.

Ideal: multitask by utilizing the hottest gadgets. We will save time and be commended for our corporate genius. Real: let us see whether our time management is actually more or less out of control.

Ideally, if Spirit could speak, it would probably tell us:
"Humans, you show a propensity for holding onto your ideals as if they were divinely ordained beliefs. You may have anointed yourselves a position as 'Supreme Thinker' among god's many creatures. Yet, many of your ideals deeply offend and trouble me. Come off your ideal wagons and passionately live *in the moment* from your hearts."

The game of life simply cannot and must not be lived based on an assortment of abstract ideals.

Although ideals are humanity's mental abstractions elevated to a status of perfection, ideally we would want our ideas to pulsate, change and adapt to suit the changing needs of humanity. Or else, our ideals end up perpetuating a culture of myths.

Chapter 73 .

Certainty

We can be certain that seeking certainty in life creates anxieties, disappointments and heartaches because we are choosing to avoid the obvious.

Certainty demands that mysteries are solved and unraveled.

In our quest for certainty, we find ingenious ways to insure our longevity and immortality.

We bolster our national security, airport screenings and military strongholds. We install the most sophisticated earthquake, tornado, hurricane and tsunami detectors. We burglarize our homes. We put up smoke alarms. We fasten seat belts. We cut down on cholesterol, refined sugars and harmful trans fats. We get regular routine medical checkups and screenings. We run anti-virus and firewall software. We expect science to provide concrete proof for our every existential issue.

These may be reassuring safeguards when it comes to matters of natural catastrophes, finance, health and the wellbeing of our children. An existential platform based on certainty, however, must be an illusion.

Certainty in life is inconclusive.

For certain, matters pertaining to Spirit cannot be proved beyond a shadow of a doubt by ordinary means. Spirit does not communicate to us—written, oral or otherwise—through coherent language.

Even if we were handed life's directions, they will still need to be decoded.

The decoder, who is human, will always influence the decoding.

Certainly, an accuracy of intent is lost in our translations of them.

And even if spiritual instructions were given to us free of obligations, the majority of us would probably not bother to read and follow all of the directions, to the letter.

Further compounding the paradox: human nature seems to have a certain propensity for editorializing, embellishing and altering, rather than following instructions exactly.

We *certainly* cannot expect to be in control of something that operates outside the realm of our ordinary perceptual senses and refuses to stay still long enough for us to figure out everything there is to know about it.

Besides, is it not the essence of all good mysteries: to keep us guessing?

In light of the perpetual motions of life, how can certainty exist?

There *are* a few matters about which we can be certain:

A gloriously wise and magnificent supreme being created the universe.

The universe is so vast; it is beyond ordinary human comprehension.

The sun is a star.

Earth is a planet.

Our sun is an ordinary star among billions of other stars and galaxies out there.

Life on Earth is dependent on the sun.

Every living thing will inevitably die.

Our ancestors worshipped the sun. They made a very ordinary star into god.

Spiritual traditions passed down to us from our ancestors must be updated based on our current views of our place in the universe.

Of these matters, we can be certain.

Certainly, as a sign of our gratitude, we must live our lives with passion and purpose.

Certainly, the rest we will have to leave as mysteries.

Chapter 74.

Boredom

When certainty, idealism, perfection and magic sap the spontaneity out of a person's soul, boredom sets in.

Let us begin playing the game of boredom by admitting we are bored.

Our 9 to 5 jobs may bore us. We would rather start our own business.

Our life partners may bore us. We would rather trade him or her in for a more suitable model.

Our mental noises may bore us. We would rather hear the strong, steady and purposeful beats of our hearts.

Our constant anxieties may bore us. We would rather feel intuitive and confident in our world views.

Our environments may bore us. We would rather live close to nature than in a 54-story high-rise on Fifth Avenue.

Our spiritual babbling may bore us. We would rather speak truthfully and without inhibitions.

Our money situation may bore us. We have too much, and we would rather give it away. We have too little, and we would rather be unconditionally awarded beyond our wildest imagination.

Our lifestyle may bore us. We would rather move out of the cities and suburbs.

Our emails, text messages, and Internet relationships may bore use. We would rather throw out all modern gadgets and move to a deserted island.

Our stacks of folders and piles of paper may bore us. We would rather put them in the incinerator.

Our friends may bore us. We would rather sail solo around the world.

Our family may bore us. We would rather adopt an entire tribe of total strangers from an underdeveloped corner of the globe who would truly appreciate a kind and lending hand.

Our political views may bore us. We would rather run for office and change the world one baby step at a time.

Our patterns may bore us. We would rather change.

Our life may bore us. We would rather intimately connect with Spirit.

If only we knew how?

With this admission, our boredom sets in, again.

The magical thing about a genuinely intimate contact with Spirit is that life is so amazing, exciting and awesome, we would not waste our time being boring.

Chapter 75.

Indulgence

Instead of politically correct, it is fashionable to be spiritual correct these days. Have you noticed that spirituality has become fodder for gurus of fashionable lifestyle trends?

Meditation, yoga and spa retreats to exotic destinations. Hundreds of designer diets all claiming to be more effective than the next. Herbal remedies for staying the process of aging. Designer chocolates, teas, potions, lotions and aromatherapy candles claiming medicinal and healing properties. Antioxidant enhanced waters, a chocolate named "Bliss" and grapefruit, lemongrass essences in soaps. Organic, free range, macrobiotic and raw food sources. Foreign sounding treatments given in a light ambience of incense by mystical healers with foreign accents. All promising us an easy attainment of spiritual wellbeing.

It would appear that even our souls can be "styled" these days.

Taking something that is as sacred as life and using it to brand sensual pleasures for the sake of making money is indulgent.

Indulgence is not merely a topic meant to titillate our sensual side. At issue here again are existential context and perspective.

First: our over-indulgence can kill, if indulgence is viewed to be more important than being alive.

Second: have no doubt that many people are willing to compromise a genuinely spiritual exploration at the expense of keeping up their self-indulgent choices in lifestyle.

Third: when push comes to shove, common sense tell us that no amount of green tea, antioxidants and positive thinking can be expected to boost a depleted immune system, if, very simply and very basically, the body has not gotten enough restful sleep.

Fourth: when real survival, meaning life or death, is at stake, those of us who can only gather enough grains to make a weak porridge to stay the bloated bellies of starving children would not care if our food source is organic or mass produced?

When we are self-centered, self-absorbed and live life seeking sensual pleasures and avoiding psychic pains, we cannot help ourselves but be indulgent in our life choices.

From Spirit's perspective, it did not inspire us with life so that we fill our lives with the latest and hippest must-have consumable goods. Because what is more important: breathing or a designer's label?

Look around us. Are we paying lip service to fashionable styles over spiritual substance or substance over style?

Are spiritually-based lifestyle trends marketing authentic choices in life?

Have some of us forsaken Spirit for our indulgences—in substance, essence and existence?

Although spiritual mystique and allure can be tastefully bottled, packaged, styled and sold, spiritual truths cannot.

Let me speak clearly and directly: An authentic and personal exploration into the mysteries of Spirit cannot be packaged, styled and sold.

As spiritual fads come and go with the changing tides of popularity polls, humanity's eternal quest to realize spiritual intimacy is here to stay for as long as human beings care to be around.

Chapter 76.

Competition

To the delight of avenging egos worldwide, the game of competition seems to consume our undivided attention.

In nature, competition ensures that the fittest survive. By outlasting another member of the same species, genes for the survival of the fittest are passed onto subsequent generations. In this way, survival machines are programmed by natural selection to realize a competitive spirit.

I learn plenty about human social conditioning from my observations of canine behavior. My two large-breed male dogs, for example, are constantly jockeying for the top dog position. Who can run the fastest, gnaw on the biggest bone, keep the best toys, fetch the most balls, gain the most affection, be the first in and out of the front, car and porch doors and shower me with the sloppiest kisses. From my observations of them, I have come to realize that competition is innately a primal, and fairly base, instinct.

In this game, human beings are no exception.

How we love to compete. The topic will easily fill an entire book. Two vantage points are pertinent here.

First: in our socialized competitions, such as sports, game shows, reality shows, elections, beauty pageants, gambling and even philanthropy, there can be one, and only one, winner. The rest of the pack, according to the rules of engagement, must lose.

From what they see around them, our youngsters, as well as many grown-ups, might misconstrue that the primary mission in life is to "outsmart, outwit and outlast" an opponent.

In moderation and balance, healthy competition is good for the spirit. In excess, it can produce monsters of arrogance and egotism.

Egos worldwide thrive on an ample diet of competition: "I have to be the best. I have to be better than everyone else. I have to do whatever it takes to ensure that I beat all my competitors."

It may be the only way ego knows to numb psychic shame.

When competition is instigated primarily by the personality, we have people whose successes in life depends on the approval of others. As a consequence, values tend to be plastic, superficial and shallow because they haven't the depth of character to compete from a place of selfhood.

Life is hard enough. Why would players from the same team want to compete against one another? And which life team player is really in charge of the game: ego, personality or self?

Competing for the sole purpose of winning presents a conflict in existential values.

Simply put, life is not a contest. Winning is not the benchmark for having played the game of life well. Ultimately, in life, there are no winners or losers—only how well one has lived one's life.

As modern gladiators, we must be willing to compete from a place of heart.

When competition is under the guardianship of the self, the game of competition can take on the character of joyful play (see Chapter 31), rather than a means to the end. An intimate connection with Spirit facilitates spiritual maturity, such that we gain the perspective: that competition is just a game.

Second: Not only is competition hardwired into our instincts to survive, but modern life completes for our time, attention and energy. For example, how many spirituality, self-help and how to books are published today versus 10 years ago? How many tens of thousands of books in general—fictions, nonfictions, textbooks and children's books—are published annually? Then, there are the text messages, emails, cell phone calls, websites, cable channels, cross-continental travel, video conferences, piles of paper, brands of cars, denims, tennis shoes, sunglasses, moisturizers, breakfast cereals, detergents, teas, coffees, chocolates, scheduled appointments, gym time, yoga time, up time, down time, me time, and simply no time to breath; all competing for our attention.

Many of us suffer from short attention spans. We have become an attention deficit society. No wonder the media introduces mega loads of entertaining twists.

This is the real world we live in.

As such, this book must be relevant.

For that matter, any spiritual exploration must be relevant.

Why? Few of us have the luxury of secluding ourselves in a remote Himalayan cave humming and chanting for 15 years to "figure out" life and where we fit in. That brand of spiritual practice belongs to bygone eras and transplanted alien cultures

But also for the simple reason that, as its author, I want to make a difference in people's live. (The whole time I was writing this book, I kept one mantra going: "Self, make it compelling enough because you are competing with the Great Big Matrix for your readers' attention.")

Our world has drastically changed. Spirituality must follow suit.

Chapter 77.

Challenges

The self, with the spirited support of each life player (soul, Spirit, observing self, ego, superego and personality) has this to say about life:

"Knock me down.

I know with unwavering conviction that, not only will I get back up, each time I right myself, I grow more resolute.

I have a backbone.

Not only do I have a backbone; it is a strong one.

I can meet any obstacles head on and not back down from what life throws at me.

I am continually being told such-and-such cannot be done; not do this or not do that; not think this or that; and not trust this or that.

I know because it has happened so many countless times; I have lost count.

I am squarely planted and firmly rooted on my own two feet.

Like a willow tree that sways with the gentlest of summer breezes, I know without a doubt I will not break or snap during a torrential monsoon.

Like an ever-pliable rubber band, my spirit has an incredible capacity to stretch and bend.

Try as it might, life cannot break my spirit.

I courageously carry on.

I am set on carrying on.

I am not afraid.

I am not even afraid of death.

My intimate contact with Spirit helps me feel secure—here on Earth and into whatsoever world I will inevitably re-visit when I die.

I know I will face my share of hardships, strive, suffering and struggles in life—in my health, relationships, family, job, accidents, death and loss of those dear to me.

I have experienced my share of challenges in life.

How I deal with them is what makes me unique."

Having a solid spiritual foundation is what helps us get through life's inevitable ups and downs.

Lord knows, the game of life *is* full of challenges. Yet, there are those among us who possess a resiliency for transforming life's challenges into opportunities of personal enrichment.

The more spiritually developed and mature, the better the existential coping mechanisms are in place for dealing with life's many challenges.

People who have such a spiritual foundation exhibit greater resilience and agility. Even in strive, they find peace and solace.

They are completely being real and authentic. It is not an act they put on.

Wholeheartedly, they accept that one of the purposes of life is to face and conquer each and every challenge that life throws at us.

How have *you* dealt with the many challenges that life has thrown your way?

How would you want to deal with life's many challenges?

Do you consider dealing with life's challenges a kind of play or is it a tedious chore for you?

How has life's challenges deepened or isolated you from Spirit?

Do you view life's challenges as a kind of mysterious game life requires us to play or a form of punishment?

Which game theories, game strategies or game plans do you practice?

Our individual answers and views determine the way we think and live.

Whichever game plan, strategy and/or game theory we practice dictate the kind of results and consequences we can expect in how we meet life's many challenges.

This special grace that is bestowed on humanity is also the same path to selfhood that predominantly challenges the greater majority of us.

Act 14 .

Rise Above the Crowd

Ask heart for answers.

Chapter 78 .

Care in Living

Care begins the process; everything else follows.
Deciding to care instantaneously alters the path of lives.

Care is the glue that unites and marries us to Spirit, to the extent that there is no separation, isolation, division or divorce—to life itself.

We care that our spiritual life is as important, if not more so, than our life styles.

We care about others because we are all in the same boat.

We care that our existence validates and values other lives.

We care that we do unto others as we would ourselves.

We care that we do unto ourselves as we would others.

We care *about* ourselves because, without an intact and functional self, we would have not the self-reliance to care for or about others.

We care *for* ourselves because we realize that, before any of us can authentically care for another, we must all be responsible for taking the best care that we are capable, of ourselves

We care that we live life passionately.

We care that we live life creatively, rather than remotely.

We care that we have dreams.

We care that our dreams come true.

We care that we have creative outlets for our inspirations.

We care that our existence is meaningful and purposeful.

We care that, at the end of our lives, we know without a doubt: we will have left a constructive and lasting mark on society.

With care, Spirit becomes our most intimate partner and companion in life.

We care that we develop spiritually.

We care that we grow spiritually.

We care that we mature spiritually.

We care that we develop psychologically.

We care that we grow psychologically.

We care that we mature psychologically.

Care is the motivating emotion that compels us to explore Spirit.

We care that we develop emotionally.

We care that we grow emotionally.

We care that we mature emotionally.

We care that we develop mentally.

We care that we grow mentally.

We care that we mature mentally.

We care that we develop physically.

We care that we grow physically.

We care that we mature physically.

With spiritually development, growth and maturity, we acquire the *capacity* to compassionately care for others and the world.

Care is the glue that binds us to our spiritual nature.

With care, Spirit becomes our most intimate partner and companion in life.

With care, we cannot divorce ourselves from life.

Care softens the exploration. With care, the quest becomes less about whether we solve the mystery or not and more about caring for life itself.

We pass our caring onto our children, so that they will develop, grow and mature in all respects.

Our caring generates a ripple effect—in our personal lives

and in the world.

The ripple quietly spreads out into the world that we all belong to and live in.

We care that we are connected to one another by a common link.

We care that we are human.

In this way, our caring intimately touches the many spirits and souls who have chosen to take human form.

To care, all it takes is a decision.

Chapter 79.

Mindful Living

We take care to be mindful.

Mindful living requires us to be disciplined and consistent in our conscious attention.

Cognition is not an idea. A person may be cognitive of the word "awareness". Yet, to be cognizant of being aware takes more than just knowing the word as vocabulary. We must follow through our cognition with a lived action.

In life, "having thoughts" is not a prerequisite or indicator of mindfulness. A mind full of over-intellectualizations, ideals and noisy chatter cannot be mindful.

Existential ambivalence is a waste of our mind's energies. Spirit cannot afford to be hesitant as it animates us with its life force. A "yes" from Spirit means there is life. A "no" means life will end.

Train the mind to decide on a simple "yes" or an emphatic "no". Then take the mental decision for what a "yes" and a "no" is really worth in life. Use them; apply them; attend to them and act on them in life. Affirmations and negations that come forth from our gut instinct and common sense are deserving of our full attention. Do not deliberate, argue, resist, give excuses, explain or analyze the situation to death. The answer has been given: it is either a "yes" or a "no".

We care that in our thoughts, we feel confident and secure about life, rather than fearful or anxious.

Mindful living seeks to modulate a balance between our instinct, intellect and inhibitions.

In mindful living, we activate our conscious control to override our undesirable primal impulses. We realize that ego cannot be expected to manage primal impulses because ego and id are the two divisions of the psyche. It would be like asking the left arm to control the right leg. Such a feat would cause horrendous migraines.

Yet, in our minds, we are also cognizant of the parallel reality that a great majority of our primal impulses are not entirely undesirable. Many are in place to ensure our survival.

In mindful living, rather than denying, avoiding, ignoring or repressing, the conscious mind concedes to the unconscious mind because the unconscious is the alter ego of the conscious. Like the two faces of a coin, their conjoined union makes for mindful living.

The primary intent of mindful living is to intimately connect with the life-giving force that graces our minds with the possibility of life.

The conscious mind graciously concedes to Spirit as a force to be reckoned with. As such, the mind must avail itself to Spirit rather than hinder Spirit's animating obligations.

Let the mind remember its place.

In mindful living, the mind—conscious and unconscious—concedes to the self. Both aspects of the mind have developed the spiritual awareness that a mind's purpose is to serve the self and not the other way around.

Spiritual intimacy requires mental calmness, peace and silence. Serenity enables the mind and Spirit to existentially hum their tunes of life in harmony.

The human mind is a wonderful creation.

We ought to be proud of it.

Our mindful choices reflect a respect of our being alive for very specific spiritual purposes.

Chapter 80.

Responsible Living

We care to be self accountable.

Self-responsibility begins with a personal decision.

The decision takes the form of a promise—to one's self.

This silent promise, which manifests itself as a life decision, requires mental discipline.

To be mentally disciplined, we accept responsibility for those twists in our psyches, regardless of how they came to be there.

We promise self to be responsible that we are not overly dependent on others.

We promise self to be responsible that we are not overly dependent on others for our intimate contact with Spirit.

We promise self to be responsible that our egos do not abuse our positions of power.

We promise self to be responsible that our words match our actions.

We promise self to be responsible that our words match our intentions.

We promise self to be responsible that our word choices and intentions begin with fundamentals and basics.

We promise self to be responsible for our psychic delusions and distortions.

We promise self to be responsible for those inadvertent twists in fate.

We promise self to be responsible for every action.

The self is spiritually mature enough to accept responsibility for its actions and consequences. When we accept responsibility for the consequences of our action, we have no one to blame but ourselves.

Responsible living requires us to be mindful.

To live our lives responsibly requires each of us to realize the purpose for which Spirit invested its energies in each unique human form.

We realize that:

The self accepts responsibility for maintaining psychic wholeness.

The self realizes that the id, ego and superego are aspects of its psychic constitution.

The self is responsible for managing the id, ego and superego.

The self is responsible for living.

No one is exempt from self-responsibility.

Spiritual responsibility is not something that can be externally validated or measured. The responsibility is accepted at a deeply core and personal level.

In this way, we are required to be accountable to no one but ourselves.

With responsible living, we mature spiritually.

Chapter 81.

Courageous Living

Our spiritual nature cannot be disposed of.

It takes courage to admit we are not perfect; because then, we are not living a fantasy.

It takes courage to own up to denial; because then, we can factually identify our problem areas.

It takes courage to admit we are screwed up; because then, we can go about fixing ourselves.

It takes courage to honestly face our deepest pains; because then, instead of expecting others to fix or rescue us, we can heal ourselves.

It takes courage to grow up—emotionally and psychologically; because then, we are mature enough to take care of ourselves.

It takes courage to stand out.

It takes courage to stand apart from the crowd.

It takes courage to voice our inalienable personal truth.

It takes courage to stand up for what we believe in.

It takes courage to resist popular trends.

It takes courage to question conventions.

It takes courage to revolt against tradition.

It takes courage to admit ignorance, oblivion and/or resistance in life.

It takes courage to ask for help.

It takes courage to act on gut instinct and common sense.

It takes courage to speak honestly from our hearts.

It takes courage to say "yes". It takes courage to say, "no, thank you."

With a simple, yet emphatic "yes" or "no", we courageously sort through our choices in life.

It takes courage to live one's own life.

It takes courage to live life fully.

It takes courage to live the life we were meant to live, rather than pleasing or pacifying everyone around us.

Courageous living requires gut-wrenching emotional honesty and a promise to be accountable to no one but ourselves.

We proudly and openly show every hard-earned battle scar and wound for the whole world to see. We have mastered courageous living.

Master courageous living and the game of life takes on a completely novel character.

The game becomes fun.

Rather than feeling as if we are being played, we know we can be in charge of our destiny.

It takes courage to accept responsibility for what has happened to us—good and bad; because then, we reclaim control over our destinies.

We courageously concede that we are the creators of our own existential demons and monsters. We are our own worst spiritual enemy.

Live courageously from our hearts in a way that matches our words.

Time does not wait for us and we get only one chance in this life.

Chapter 82.

Existential Values

In life, and in death, what constitutes value?

What makes one life more or less worthy than another's?

What makes one person's life purpose more or less worthy than another's?

Humanity's tendency for making subjective judgments is more commonplace than we would like to admit.

A statement of fact, for example regarding value, left to its own devices is merely a statement of fact.

What we *choose* to do with facts is what makes facts valuable in human culture.

The game of values dictates that we constantly pick and choose the standards by which we gauge every "thing" in life to be worthy or unworthy.

Let us face some simple facts:

Spirit does not need food to survive.

Spirit does not need oxygen to survive.

Spirit does not need water to survive.

Just as U2-384, Spirit, knows not commerce.

Spirit has no use for our money.

What would Spirit do with money? Put a down payment on its next incarnation? If so, at what price and pay to whom?

An intimate contact with Spirit ensures that we value what may not immediately appear to be pleasant or pleasurable at face value.

Value is more than just good or bad. For example, is it good or bad that Spirit does not need food, oxygen, water, clothes or money to survive?

The fact is: good-bad, positive-negative, black-white are not profoundly deep spiritual values. As categories of values, good-bad, positive-negative, black-white may be appropriate for 2-year olds; but they severely limit our choices in life, because the simplicity of our words do not reflect the complexities, minutiae and multiple nuances of life.

Appearances can be deceiving. Living by permitting the personality filter or ego to make good-bad, positive-negative or black-white choices in life values can lead to an existence devoid of substance and value.

At which point, the person must expend valuable time, energy and resources to rediscover his/her authentic self in the rubbles of personas s/he has gotten so used to showing the world that s/he forgot that a persona is not "who I am".

A life devoid of existential values creates excruciating pain.

Values must be *vitally* important.

Value must be substantive.

Each and every human life *matters.*

We care that life is precious.

Spiritual values are broader than faith- or politically-based values. Because when we value life, we value all life—not just of the human sort.

An intimate contact with Spirit ensures that we value life—period.

Using the terms and concepts presented in this introduction, more thorough discussions about life values will be presented in the next three volumes of this series.

Chapter 83 .

In the End

God forbid if we were to die in the next instant.
What would be our final thoughts?
Would we be prepared for death?
Do we have faith? Or at least, trust that our physical death does not represent the final ending?
Are we proud or saddened by the life that we lived?
In the final moment, would we be afraid?
In the final moment, would the mind chronicle through an account of our biographical histories?
Would we have more regrets than accomplishments?
What are our regrets?
What are our accomplishments?
Do our regrets outweigh our accomplishments, or vice versa?
How well were we loved by others?
How many people would attend our funerals?
Did we leave a legacy, permanent record or distinctive mark on earth?
In the final moment, would we be alone or would we feel the presence of other spirits?
Do we feel confident about where we are headed next?
In the face of death, can we realize what was truly important and valuable in life and what was mere trivia?
How do we deal with such thoughts and feelings in our last

hours?

Where did we learn that it takes hard work to change?

Having come to the end of this introductory exploration, can you honestly admit the spiritual stage of development you are at?

Do not hide from the truth.

Hiding from truth shrouds existential mysteries behind a facade of cowardly complacency and apathy.

This only postpones the inevitable fallout when the darkest and deepest secrets in a life are disclosed.

Before we can expect to fly, we must begin every spiritual journey by taking one small step closer to authentically living from a place of Spirit.

Chapter 84.

Decision

Virtually every single person who experiences a spiritual awakening attests to a profound personal transformation: in his or her convictions and purpose in life.

They feel as though life is no longer a mysterious force that must be wrangled with. Life feels rich and purposeful.

The game turns a corner. Instead of feeling as though they must adopt an adversary position in life, they feel a sense of relief. They are having loads of fun while fully engaged in playing the game.

They find grace.

When we realize an intimate contact with Spirit, we are enlivened by an instantaneous and spontaneous awakening, which may appear miraculous.

All it takes is a decision. Not a decision about whether we want chocolate mousse or raspberry sorbet, but a life-decision.

The decision becomes a defining moment in life.

The decision demonstrates to Spirit the level of our commitment. Spirit knows that we have signed on with a fully staffed, full-time team—with all team players present, accounted for and willing to engage in the game of life.

Regardless of what life deals us, Spirit knows we will not give up.

Preparing for the last moment of life takes an entire lifetime—a lifetime of our being intimately connected with each of our spirits.

Act 15 .

Full Circle

What goes around, comes around.

Act 15.

Full Circle

Any exploration into Spirit is a mystical experience because we must rely on no one but our own intimate connections with the cosmic forces that "speaks" to us wordlessly.

Nearly 6.6 billion people inhabit the earth. Hypothetically, if three-quarters of them followed one of the mainstream religions, that still leaves 1.65 billion—that is 1,650,000,000—people who, whether by choice or circumstance, must find meaning and purpose in life on their own. If one does not choose to look to the major religions and spiritual teachings for answers, where does one turn?

Herein lies the mystery.

Words are like coins. They serve basic cultural and social purposes. Like the coins that intrigue and puzzle our alien visitor from outer space, enough words (or different coins) must be gathered, pooled and sorted before we (or the alien) can draw any conclusions or make sense of them—both of words and coins.

This first volume is an introductory exploration. The most basic concepts, terminologies, their definitions, applications and implications are introduced here. Think of it as a kind of word bank. In it, I advocate that we use:

simple;
familiar;
neutral;

and self-evident words, terms and concepts that derive from the secular and vernacular.

For although the "University of Spirit" may be explored in many different tongues, its core foundation must be universally accessible, acceptable and understandable by all. An introductory exploration into the mysteries of Spirit must be:

Substantive: meaning "substantial", as in important. "Core values are *substantive*."

Vital: meaning "necessary to life", as in sustaining and maintaining life. "Oxygen is *vital* to life."

Essential: meaning "basic", as in fundamental and indispensable to life. "Procreation is *essential* to life."

Substantive, *vital* and *essential* are further broken down as follows: Spiritual explorations and insights are innate. Spiritual explorations arise from instinctual impulses that are as basic and natural to human survival as breathing, eating and mating. They are an inherent, rather than a separate part of human nature.

Second: spiritual quest is not a privilege. It is a necessity. In other words, the process is not available nor should it only be accessible to a privileged few. It is neither extraordinary nor special. The exploration is universal and archetypal among each and every member of our species. It is as necessary to human survival as air and water, because Spirit is the life-force energy that sustains the human heart.

Third: to give Spirit a "voice".

Fourth: this series does not touch upon the topic of God.

Fifth: the exploration needs to be updated in keeping with modern life and contemporary concepts.

Sixth: to make the material as accessible to as diverse an audience as possible by demystify the subject matter of spirituality.

And lastly: it is unfitting for any one person, regardless of the spiritual position—whether it is theological, philosophical, religious and otherwise—to dictate over another person's intimate contact with Spirit.

This volume and its companion three volumes are not intended to be a stand-in as *the* definitive instruction manual on life. Nor is it making such a claim. As its author, I serve only as an advocate.

The three key words, substantive, vital and essential, and seven secondary points—innate, universal, vocally expressive, secular, relevant and unprejudicial—are encompassed in this volume, as well as the subsequent three volumes of this series on "An Intimate Contact with Humanity".

Volume II, Wings of Inspiration, Poetic Reflections on the Recovery of Spirit, explores the importance of mending and recovering a broken spirit. Before spiritual growth can occur, areas that are damaged or broken must first be carefully attended to; or else any growth spurts in spirit will result in existential deformities.

Volume III, Free Spirit, Poetic Reflections on the Growth of Spirit, explores the topic of spiritual growth.

Volume IV, E-M-Power, Poetic Reflections on the Maturation of Spirit, explores the topic of spiritual maturity. Before maturity can take place, adequate development and growth must first be in place; or else maturation will be mismatched relative to the mental, physical and psychoemotional capabilities and tolerance levels of the individual.

This series of four titles is written for all human beings. Its intent is to encourage personal exploration.

In our humanity, we are united by a common bond. Our spiritual nature unites every one of us by this bond. Some of us choose to explore outside the context of organized religion. It is mainly for these people—but as well as those who are guided by their faith—that this book and its three subsequent volumes will captivate an audience.

Human beings are mysterious creatures. We believe that something significant and magnificent exists outside the purely physical realm of reality.

Spiritual quests are lofty affairs.

But, before our spirits can soar into the heavenly skies, we must advance forward by taking small baby steps with both our feet firmly planted on the surface of the planet.

Lest in our haste, we omit or commit careless errors of monumental proportions which may inadvertently take human cultures eons of time to rectify and recover from.

Hopefully, these four volumes bring poetic justice to the complexities, mysteries and beauty of Spirit.

You only have to look into your soul to know your true spiritual nature.

Acknowledgement

I thank Dr. John Upledger, D.O., O.M.M., for planting a grain of sand in the unsuspecting pearl of my consciousness which invariably germinated into this series on the soulful purposes of our spiritual nature.

Barbara Chang serves as CEO and founder of Destiny Technologies®. She specializes in simplifying and demystifying ancient spiritual traditions, and adapts them for practical use in contemporary popular culture.

She can be reached at www.destinytechnologies.org, email: info@destinytechnologies.com. Or write her at P.O. Box 1707, Big Bear City, CA 92314-1707.

Look for her forthcoming books:

- *The Body's Poetry in Motion: Integrating Biomechanical Systems with Bioenergies;*

- *Legacy of Sacred Mothership: A Modern Women's Guide to Power Icons of the Female Mystique;*

- *Wings of Inspiration: Poetic Reflections on the Recovery of Spirit;*

- *Free Spirit: Poetic Reflections on the Growth of Spirit;*

- *E-M-Power: Poetic Reflections on the Maturation of Spirit;* and

- *Birth Trauma: The Long-Term Bioenergetic Effects on Health & Wellbeing*

in your local bookstores.

Destiny Technologies® promotes education and training in the advancement of self-improvement, holistic healing and human evolution. It is registered with the United States Patent and Trademark Office. (Unsolicited sales are not welcomed and will be promptly dismissed.)

CPSIA information can be obtained at www.ICGtesting.com
Printed in the USA
LVOW041108280712

291970LV00001B/14/P